Pearson Education
AP® Test Prep Series

AP® English Language and Composition
to accompany

WRITING
AMERICA

LANGUAGE AND COMPOSITION IN CONTEXT

AP® Edition

Steven F. Jolliffe

St. Johnsbury Academy

PEARSON

Boston   Columbus   Indianapolis   New York   San Francisco   Upper Saddle River
Amsterdam   Cape Town   Dubai   London   Madrid   Milan   Munich   Paris   Montreal   Toronto
Delhi   Mexico City   São Paulo   Sydney   Hong Kong   Seoul   Singapore   Taipei   Tokyo

Senior Sponsoring Editor: Katharine Glynn
Senior Development Editor: Marion Castellucci
Senior Supplements Editor: Donna Campion
Project Manager: Teresa Ward
Electronic Page Make-up: Grapevine Publishing Services, Inc.
Cover Production: Alison Barth Burgoyne
Manufacturing Buyer: Roy Pickering
Production Manager: Alicia Orlando
Text and Cover Printer: Edwards Brothers

2 3 4 5 6 7 8 9 10—EBM—15 14 13

www.pearsonschool.com/advanced

ISBN-10:   0-133-25892-0
ISBN-13: 978-0-133-25892-9

Table of Contents

About Your Pearson AP® Guide

Pearson Education is the leading publisher of textbooks worldwide. With operations on every continent, we make it our business to understand the changing needs of students at every level, from kindergarten to college. We think that makes us especially qualified to offer this series of AP® test prep books, tied to some of our best-selling textbooks.

Our reasoning is that as you study for your course, you're preparing along the way for the AP® test. If you can tie the material in the book directly to the test you'll be taking, it makes the material that much more relevant and enables you to focus your time most efficiently. And that's a good thing!

The AP® exam is an important milestone in your education. A high score means you're in a better position for college acceptance, and possibly puts you a step ahead with college credits. Our goal is to provide you with the tools you need to excel on the exam . . . the rest is up to you.

Good luck!

Preface

As a student in an Advanced Placement (AP®) Language and Composition class, you probably have some questions about how the whole AP® program works and how it can benefit you. Also, since you will probably be taking an AP® Language and Composition Examination, and you want to find out more about it. This book will help you in several important ways. The first part of this book introduces you to the AP® Language and Composition course and the AP® Language and Composition Examination. You'll learn helpful details about the exam, the testing experience, and your released scores. in simpler terms, this part of the book provides critical information regarding the administration of the exam, although it does offer a brief snapshot of the exam itself.

In Part II of this book you will examine the multiple-choice section of the AP® exam. In this section, you will familiarize yourself with the multiple choice question formats, find many test-taking strategies (notably annotating strategies), review key terms, and practice your skills on a number of sample multiple-choice reading passages.

Part III of this book gives you assistance in responding to the three types of writing prompts found on the AP® exam: the analysis, argumentative, and synthesis prompts. You will explore strategies including T-Charts, the Rhetorical Box, and Rhetorical Parts to help in your response to the exam's analysis essay. You will also be introduced to organizational tools designed to help prepare a quality response to both the synthesis and argumentative essays. This section also offers you tools for approaching visuals, charts, and citations. Finally, this section gives you practice in responding to sample essay prompts. These are followed by answers and explanations to help you understand how to acheive a quality response.

Finally, in Part IV, you will find two full-length sample exams. These will help you practice taking the exam under real-life testing conditions. The more familiar you are with the AP® Language and Composition Exam ahead of time, the more comfortable you'll be on testing day.

We would like to acknowledge James Butler from Kealakehe High School in Kealakekua, Hawaii, for his valuable input.

Section I

Introduction to the AP® English Language and Composition

This section gives an overview of the Advanced Placement program and the AP® English Language and Composition. Part I gives information about exam protocol, outlines the goals of the AP® Language and Composition course, and provides a preview to the types of questions you will encounter on the exam. Review Part I carefully before trying the sample test items in Part II and Part III.

The Advanced Placement Program

The AP® Program is sponsored by the College Board, a nonprofit organization that oversees college admissions examinations. The AP® Program offers thirty-three college-level courses to qualified high school students. If you receive a grade of 3 or higher on an AP® exam, you may be eligible for college credit, depending on the policies of the institution you plan to attend. Over 3,000 colleges and universities around the world grant credit to students who have performed well on AP® exams. Some institutions grant sophomore status to incoming first-year students who have demonstrated mastery of several AP® subjects. You can check the policies of specific institutions on the College Board's website (www.college-board.com). In addition, the College Board confers a number of AP® Scholar Awards on students who score 3 or higher on three or more AP® exams. Additional awards are available to students who receive very high grades on four or five AP® exams.

Why Take an AP® Course?

You may be taking an AP® course simply because you like challenging yourself and you are thirsty for knowledge. Another reason may be that you know that colleges look favorably on applicants who have AP® courses on their secondary school transcripts. AP® classes involve rigorous, detailed lessons, a lot of homework, and numerous tests. College admissions officers may see your willingness to take these courses as evidence of your work ethic and commitment to your education. Because AP® course work is more difficult than average high school work, many admissions officers evaluate AP® grades on a higher academic level. For example, if you receive a B in an AP® class, it might carry the same weight as an A in a regular-level high school class.

Your AP® English Language and Composition course prepares you for many of the skills you will need to succeed in college. For example, your teacher will have you read a variety of works of non-fiction that will challenge your comprehension and analytical skills. Additionally, you will be asked to write persuasive, well-styled essays utilizing rhetorical strategies of your own design. AP® Literature and Composition teachers routinely give substantial reading assignments, and students develop an appreciation of how authors use language and rhetorical strategies to craft meaning and persuade their audience. By studying the rhetorical strategies and structures of a variety of non-fiction works, you will gain a deeper appreciation and greater understanding of effective works of persuasion. This depth of understanding will serve you well as you enter college.

Each college or university decides whether or not to grant college credit for an AP® course, and each bases this decision on what it considers satisfactory grades on AP® exams. Depending on what college you attend and what area of study you pursue, your decision to take the AP® English Language and Composition Examination could save you tuition money. You can contact schools directly to find out their guidelines for accepting AP® credits, or use the College Board's online feature, "AP® Credit Policy Info."

Taking an AP® Examination

The AP® English Language and Composition Examination is given annually in May. Your AP® teacher or school guidance counselor can give you information on how to register for an AP® exam. Remember, the deadline for registration and payment of exam fees is usually in March, two months before the actual exam date in May. The cost of the exam is subject to change and can differ depending on the number of exams taken. However, in 2013, a single exam costs $89. For students who can show financial need, the College Board will reduce the price by $28, and your school might also waive its regular rebate of $8, so the lowest possible total price is $53. Moreover, schools in some states are willing to pay the exam fee for the student. If you feel you may qualify for reduced rates, ask your school administrators for more information.

The exams are scored in June. In mid-July, the results will be sent to you, your high school, and any colleges or universities you indicated on your answer sheet. If you want to know your score as early as possible, you can get it (for an additional charge of $8) beginning July 1 by calling the College Board at (888) 308-0013. On the phone, you'll be asked to give your AP® number, your social security number, your birth date, and a credit card number.

If you decide that you want your score sent to additional colleges and universities, you can fill out the appropriate information on your AP® Grade Report (which you will receive by mail in July) and return it to the College Board. There is an additional charge of $15 for each additional school that will receive your AP® score.

On the other hand, if a feeling of disaster prevents you from sleeping on the nights following the exam, you could choose to withhold or cancel your grade. (Withholding is temporary, whereas canceling is permanent.) Grade withholding carries a $10 charge per college or university, whereas canceling carries no fee. You'll need to write to (or e-mail) the College Board and include your name, address, gender, birth date, AP® number, the date of the exam, the name of the exam, a check for the exact amount due, and the name, city, and state of the college(s) from which you want the score withheld. You should check the College Board website for the deadline for withholding your score, but it's usually in mid-July. It is strongly suggested that you *do not* cancel your scores, since you won't know your score until mid-July. Instead, relax and try to assume that the glass is half full. At this point, you have nothing to lose and a lot to gain.

If you would like to get back your free-response booklet for a post-exam review, you can send another check for $7 to the College Board. You'll need to do this by mid-September. Finally, if you have serious doubts about the accuracy of your score for the multiple-choice section, the College Board will re-score it for an additional $25.

AP® English Language and Composition: Course Goals

The course is founded upon focused readings from a variety of historical periods and disciplines. While each instructor may have different preferences for reading selections and writing styles, the course mandates a wide array of perspectives and voices. While the exam focuses primarily on works of non-fiction, your instructor may choose—and should choose—some works of fiction to include in the course curriculum. The significant difference, however, between a study in language and composition and a study of literature is that your study of language will primarily focus on a work's rhetorical value and not its literary value. In other words, a study in language and composition focuses on argument and the ways in which unique arguments—and the strategies employed in them to persuade—are developed depending on purpose and audience. You will, therefore, read a variety of verbal and visual arguments (graphs, charts, political cartoons, etc.) that will help you to gain an appreciation for the choices and decisions the writer (or artist) has made in crafting his or her message. You will learn to ask sophisticated questions of the texts and interpret the answers with acute, responsible analysis.

The three main elements of the approach to such a study involve the rhetorical analysis of non-fiction works, the ability to synthesize ideas and information from a variety of resources, and the facility to use multiple modes of writing to address a variety of audiences. Rhetorical analysis involves a close examination of the tropes and schemes utilized by writers in developing a persuasive essay. They are the devices that develop trust, instill emotion, and illuminate logic. Synthesis is the process of examining multiple ideas and arguments in developing something new and fresh. Much of this course is designed to introduce you to a variety of viewpoints with the hope that you will be able to synthesize key elements in formulating and defending your own position on various issues. Finally, you will write frequently in this course. More importantly, however, you will explore a number of modes of writing and write for a variety of audiences and purposes. Your ability to utilize rhetorical strategies and to synthesize ideas plays a critical role in your ability to write effectively.

Additionally, significant emphasis is placed on developing your "voice" and style as a writer. Understanding how to structure, develop, and articulate a thoughtful and persuasive piece of writing is certainly a foundation of the course. To achieve this goal, instructors offer a wide range of vocabulary and terms for study, in addition to the specific modes of expression and argumentation. Acquiring and developing these writing skills will come with practice and revision; in the writing process, a premium is placed on revision and drafting.

There are, of course, other goals to a study in language and composition. For instance, you will also be asked to use the conventions of standard written English effectively and to know how to interpret information presented in footnotes and citations, among other things.

To help guide and evaluate your development as a reader and writer, your instructor may occasionally have you work with AP® English Language Released Exams. The multiple-choice sections will test your close-reading skills and understanding of important rhetorical terms and principles. These exams also offer opportunities for "timed writes," situations that closely mimic the AP®

testing environment. These opportunities will provide you exposure to each of the three prompts provided on the AP® Language and Composition Examination: the analysis prompt, the argument prompt, and the synthesis prompt. Many instructors will use these three types of prompts as a first draft that you will build into longer, more developed essays.

Understanding the AP® Language and Composition Examination

The AP® Language and Composition Examination takes three and a quarter hours. The exam probably looks like many other tests you've taken. It is made up of a multiple-choice section and a free-response (essay) section. The exam consists of 60 minutes for multiple-choice questions followed by 135 minutes of free-response questions (of which, 15 minutes is designated as a reading period). Performance on the free-response section of the exam counts for 45 percent of the total score; performance on the multiple-choice section, 55 percent. At the core of the examination are questions designed to measure your reading comprehension, analytical skills, and written expression.

Section I: Multiple-Choice Questions

Section I contains around 55 multiple-choice questions that test reading comprehension and literary analysis. You will have 60 minutes to complete Section I. The multiple-choice questions will come from a variety of non-fiction passages such as speeches, letters, histories, etc. Depending on the length of the individual passages, you will be given 4 or 5 specific passages with 10–15 questions each. This portion of the exam is followed by a 5–10 minute break—the only official break during the examination. The directions for the multiple-choice section of the test are straightforward and similar to the following:

> **Directions:** Each of the questions or incomplete statements below is followed by five suggested answers or completions. Select the choice that best answers the question or completes the statement.

The questions will primarily test your understanding of rhetorical terms, the use of language, structure, and reading comprehension. You will be asked to deal with answers "in context" and to illustrate broader understandings of the pieces. Questions that reflect an appreciation for denotative and connotative significance and your ability to understand tone and purpose are common to the test.

> *TIP FROM THE READERS*
>
> In the past, there was a penalty for guessing, but that is eliminated beginning with the 2011 exam. *Answer every question!*
>
> While there are certainly going to be questions that you may be uncertain of, you can improve your odds on hitting the right answer. For example, if the question asks you to identify the mood of a poem, but you don't know for certain the meaning of the words "elegiac" and "satiric," you need to limit your options to improve your chances. If you known any of the other choices and can eliminate some, confidently mark your answer sheet and continue. Remember, answer every question!

Section II: Free Response

The second part of the exam consists of three essays: one synthesis prompt, one analysis prompt, and one argument prompt. You will be given a fifteen-minute reading period in which to read the prompts, specifically the documents that accompany the synthesis prompt. Following the fifteen-minute reading period, you will be given 120 minutes in which to respond to all of the three prompts. Therefore, it is recommended that you allocate 40 minutes to each essay. Performance on the free-response portion of the exam accounts for 55 percent of the total score.

Prompt #1: The Synthesis Prompt

The synthesis prompt is a relatively new addition to the AP® exam. You are expected to develop a position on a specific topic utilizing a number of passages and excerpts provided to you by the College Board. Among these sources you will find visuals, often in the form of political cartoons, charts, graphs, or photographs. Additionally, you will notice that the supporting documents offer unique and contrary positions and opinions on the topic at hand; therefore, you will need to examine them carefully before developing your own position. You are, however, required to use at least three of the resources in your response. Strong responses will provide precise and apt examples as support.

Prompt #2: The Analysis Prompt

The analysis prompt involves a prose selection chosen for its voice, tone, purpose, and argument. You task is to read and analyze the passage carefully and then compose an essay in which you examine the rhetorical strategies and devices used to develop the author's argument. A strong answer will make frequent reference to the text itself and demonstrate a strong understanding of the ways in which rhetorical devices enhance an author's message.

Prompt #3: The Argument Prompt

The argument prompt provides you with the most latitude of the three writing prompts. You will be provided with an issue—and often a brief quote to introduce it—and asked to defend, challenge or qualify your position on the issue at hand. Excellent responses will present a logical argument that utilizes a number of rich, apt examples from such areas as history, literature, current events, or personal experiences.

All of these writing prompts, as well as the multiple-choice section, are examined more thoroughly in the two sections that follow.

Section II

Preparing for the Multiple-Choice Section of the AP® Language and Composition Examination

Introduction

The AP® English Language and Composition Examination consists of approximately 55 multiple-choice questions drawn from multiple selections of nonfiction writing. These selections come from essays, letters, autobiographies, histories, or other informative texts, and you will be asked roughly 10-15 questions about each passage. It is important to note that there is no penalty for an incorrect response to a question, and you are encouraged to answer as many of the questions as possible during the 60-minute time frame. If you are methodical in your approach to reading and responding to the questions, you can and will successfully complete the multiple-choice section of the exam within the given time frame. The key, of course, is to remain focused and methodical.

The goal, then, of this section of the test prep book is to provide you with a number of strategies that will be helpful in successfully completing the multiple-choice section of the AP® English Language and Composition Exam. The more you know about the exam, its structure, the types of questions you will be asked, and the ways in which to approach both passages and questions, the more confident you will be on exam day.

Types of Multiple-Choice Questions

While each individual passage will clearly generate unique questions of varying difficulty based on the intricacies of the text in question, there are generally five types of multiple-choice questions that will be asked of you.

The first type is the **direct question.** The direct question asks a question about the text and offers five possible answers. Of these answers, one will obviously be correct. What makes AP® exams, in general, more difficult than the SAT or ACT exam, is that of the other four options, only one will appear to be clearly incorrect. In other words, all three of the additional incorrect responses will contain **distractors** that may mislead you into selecting an incorrect response. Therefore, you will need to consider each option carefully before you make your selection.

There are many variations of the direct question, but you will undoubtedly see questions corresponding to the main idea, purpose, tone, word-in-context, and pronouns and their antecedents using this question type.

The second type is a question that addresses a **specific line number** or a **specific paragraph** in the text. These questions refer to specific passages in the text and ask you to consider their relevance to the larger passage. When responding to these questions, it is always wise to examine the lines before and after the specific lines so that you can consider the context in which the lines appear, before you determine the correct response. This question type is used in a variety of ways, from testing your understanding of a vocabulary word and its contextual use, to testing your analytical ability.

A third type of question uses the words **ALL . . . EXCEPT** in the question stem. These questions can be tricky because you will need to consider all of the responses carefully before selecting the correct answer. While this question type can be used in a myriad of ways, the question type will often be used to test your understanding of literary or rhetorical terms.

The fourth type of question is the **Roman numeral** question. This question type is difficult because it has the potential to offer up to three correct responses. The best way to tackle the Roman Numeral question type is to focus first on the three options (I, II, and III) and then decide which one, two or three of them is correct. Once you have ascertained this information, you should then look to the options as listed in the letters A–E. While the College Board is utilizing this question less frequently, when it is used, it is often used to assess questions about purpose or main idea.

The fifth type of question makes use of the term **inference**. These questions ask you to draw a conclusion based on the information presented to you in the text. The questions deal with abstract concepts and ideas and, unlike the other question types, the answer cannot be clearly identified or pointed to in the text. These question types often address the speaker of the passage.

Specific Reading Strategies for the Multiple-Choice Section

There are reading strategies that will help to establish the foundation for such confidence. These strategies will help you to decode the passages and successfully attack the questions. There are no shortcuts to approaching the multiple-choice section of the exam. It is important, then, that you be an active reader and read each passage carefully to consider its critical elements:

1. You should be able to identify the **speaker**, the targeted **audience.**
2. You should be able to identify the **purpose** of the passage and its overall message or **argument.**
3. You should consider the passage's **structure** and the way in which its organization helps to articulate its message in a persuasive fashion.
4. You should be able to recognize, if not by name, then by effect, **rhetorical strategies and figures of speech** utilized within a passage.
5. Additionally, you should be able to identify the effect of **diction** and **syntax** within the selection.
6. Finally, you should be able to decode information drawn from **footnotes** or **bibliographical entries.**

Understanding the Relationship Between the Speaker and the Audience

Most likely, you will not be given specific information regarding the **speaker** or intended **audience** of a select multiple-choice passage. Instead, you will be given the time frame in which the passage was originally published and whether or not the passage is drawn from an autobiography, memoir, speech, historical text, or some other work of non-fiction. Typically, the instructions provided look like this:

Read the following passage carefully before you choose your answers.
(The following passage is excerpted from a nineteenth-century letter.)

Because so little information is provided to you, you must garner what you can about the **speaker** and the intended audience using cues from the text itself. The process of recognizing these cues is important, as you can often anticipate the questions that will be asked of you by reading the passage carefully and considering the speaker and audience thoughtfully.

As you read the selection, consider the **persona** presented in the passage. Historically, the term is drawn from theater, as a persona was literally the mask actors wore on stage to represent their dramatic character. In the literary and rhetorical worlds, the persona projects the speaker's position in and attitude toward the world in general.

There are many clues in a text that help to illuminate the persona of a given piece, among them tone and language use. However, perhaps the easiest strategy to help in illuminating the persona is to conduct a simple visualization exercise. After reading the selection, close your eyes and try to visualize the speaker. What does he or she look like? What does he or she sound like? How does he or she dress? Even ordinary questions such as, What type of car does the speaker drive (assuming cars were invented at the time of writing)? or With whom would you expect the speaker to associate? are useful in helping you to better understand the speaker.

While persona offers an understanding of a speaker's character, **tone** conveys the speaker's attitude toward subject matter. Does the passage project an impassioned attitude to its subject matter or is it reasoned and logical? Is the passage didactic or instructional in tone, or is it marked by inquiry? Is the tone whimsical or caustic? There are hundreds of specific descriptors that can be aptly used to describe the tone of a speaker toward his or her subject matter, and whether you land upon the most appropriate descriptor is irrelevant, as long as you have an understanding of the speaker's tone in the passage.

With this in mind, expect to be asked variations of the following question stems:

The speaker's tone in the passage might best be described as:
The speaker's attitude toward his subject matter might best be described as:

Identifying the intended **audience** of a passage is also critical in the analysis of a multiple-choice selection. Some selections have very specific audiences. The audience may be a singular person, as is the case with letters and other forms of written correspondence. Other selections, such as political campaign speeches, have a more diverse audience with unique and varied needs. Thus, your first goal is to determine whether your audience is, indeed, a small, targeted one, or one that is broader, composed of a more unique constituency.

Your second goal is to determine the defining characteristics of the audience. The visualization strategy used to determine the persona of a selection is also useful in identifying these characteristics. In essence, you need to consider all those factors that are the constituent parts of the audience. Consider the following questions:

1. Is the audience friendly or adversarial to the speaker?
2. What are the core beliefs and values of the audience?
3. What is the demographic of the audience? Age? Gender? Ethnicity? Education? Socio-economic standing? etc.
4. What is the audience's attitude toward the subject matter? Does the speaker hope to enlist their support or change their understanding of an issue?
5. What is the audience's understanding of the issue itself? Are they the initiated or does the author intend to enlighten them?

You will undoubtedly see a number of questions in the multiple-choice section of the AP® English Language and Composition Exam that focus both specifically and tangentially on the audience and the speaker's relationship to the audience. Specifically, you will see variations on the following stem question:

The intended audience for this passage is most likely…

Ultimately, if you are going to accurately identify the author's purpose or goal, as well as the author's central argument (and, later, how the author's use of rhetorical strategies helps to persuade the audience), you will need to carefully consider the characteristics of and relationship between the speaker and the audience.

Identifying Purpose and Argument

Having established the persona and audience of a selected passage, it is important to consider the **purpose** of the passage as a whole, identifying the explicit and implicit goals of the speaker as outlined by the entire passage. This will most certainly be manifested in a stem question such as

The speaker's primary purpose in this passage is…

In order to articulate a passage's primary purpose, you should use an infinitive phrase. By using the sign of the infinitive, -to, and a strong action verb, you can effectively express the purpose of the passage. Consider the following infinitive phrases:

The purpose of the passage as a whole is
    to instruct . . .
    to challenge . . .
    to inspire . . .
    to change . . .
    to attack . . .

In order to clearly articulate the central argument or main idea of the passage, you should consider the interplay among the persona, the audience, and the overall purpose. These components work in concert with one another to frame the central argument of the passage as a whole.

Identifying the argument is, however, one of the more difficult aspects of analysis, and so you should use the aforementioned component parts—persona, audience, and purpose—to assist in identifying and articulating the argument.

Sample Passage A:

To best demonstrate this interplay between the persona, audience, purpose and argument, let's examine a letter written to Thomas Jefferson in the late eighteenth century. The passage represents a typical excerpt you might find in the multiple-choice section of the AP® exam. Its language, particularly its formality, might pose some difficulty for many readers; however, by considering the visualization strategies mentioned in this section, it is possible to accurately identify the persona, his audience, the purpose of the passage and its overarching argument.

As you read the passage, take time to circle key words or phrases that contribute to your understanding of the persona and the audience. Use these circled words and phrases to help guide your understanding of the passage. Furthermore, underline those parts of the passage that most clearly highlight the argument being presented.

Sir, suffer me to recall to your mind that time, in which the arms and tyranny of the British crown were exerted, with every powerful effort, in order to reduce you to a state of servitude: look back, I entreat you, on the variety of dangers to which you were exposed; reflect on that time, in which
5 every human aid appeared unavailable, and in which even hope and fortitude wore the aspect of inability to the conflict, and you cannot but be led to a serious and grateful sense of your miraculous and providential preservation; you cannot but acknowledge, that the present freedom and tranquility which you enjoy you have mercifully received, and that it is the
10 peculiar blessing of Heaven.

This, Sir, was a time when you clearly saw into the injustice of a state of slavery, and in which you had just apprehensions of the horrors of its condition. It was now that your abhorrence thereof was so excited, that you publicly held forth this true and invaluable doctrine, which is worthy to be
15 recorded and remembered in all succeeding ages: ``We hold these truths to be self-evident, that all men are created equal; that they are endowed by their Creator with certain unalienable rights, and that among these are, life, liberty, and the pursuit of happiness.'' Here was a time, in which your tender feelings for yourselves had engaged you thus to declare, you were then
20 impressed with proper ideas of the great violation of liberty, and the free possession of those blessings, to which you were entitled by nature; but, Sir, how pitiable is it to reflect, that although you were so fully convinced of the benevolence of the Father of Mankind, and of his equal and impartial distribution of these rights and privileges, which he hath conferred upon
25 them, that you should at the same time counteract his mercies, in detaining by fraud and violence so numerous a part of my brethren, under groaning captivity and cruel oppression, that you should at the same time be found guilty of that most criminal act, which you professedly detested in others, with respect to yourselves.
30 I suppose that your knowledge of the situation of my brethren, is too extensive to need a recital here; neither shall I presume to prescribe methods

by which they may be relieved, otherwise than by recommending to you and all others, to wean yourselves from those narrow prejudices which you have imbibed with respect to them, and as Job proposed to his friends, "put your soul in their souls' stead;" thus shall your hearts be enlarged with kindness and benevolence towards them; and thus shall you need neither the direction of myself or others, in what manner to proceed herein.

—Benjamin Banneker's letter to Thomas Jefferson

With regard to the **persona**, you will notice the formal nature of the speaker's rhetoric. The persona repeatedly addresses his audience as "sir," projecting an air of formality and politeness. Additionally, his diction selection, words such as "tyranny," "providential," "doctrine," and "benevolence," demonstrates a heightened understanding of the English language, marking the speaker as an educated man. Furthermore, references to the Bible and biblical allusions, such as that to Job, make clear the religious nature of the speaker. Finally, the explicit reference to the speaker's "brethren," those who suffer "under groaning captivity and cruel oppression," identify him as a member of this group of oppressed people. Ideally, you were able to identify some of these words and phrases that help to elucidate the speaker. You will note that some of the references also function as literary devices or rhetorical strategies—ones we will examine further in this guide.

With regard to identifying the **audience**, it is clear that this passage is written to a specific individual: Thomas Jefferson. However, you should strive to identify the specific qualities of the audience to which the speaker hopes to appeal. In the first paragraph alone, the speaker "entreats" his audience to "suffer" his argument. These words highlight the fact that Banneker's audience, Thomas Jefferson, is in a position of power and has the ability to influence the change outlined in the speaker's argument. Given the fact that the letter's recipient was, indeed, Thomas Jefferson, a well-known founding father and the author of the Declaration of Independence, Banneker is wise to quote from Jefferson's own words. He quotes a passage from the Declaration to commend his audience for his stance against oppression in the past. Furthermore, Banneker makes multiple appeals to Jefferson by referencing his own profession of faith in the endowment of liberties by a "Creator," indicating to the readers the audience's values and belief system.

This in essence leads to one of the fundamental **purposes** of the letter, which is ultimately to persuade Thomas Jefferson to apply the logic used in the Declaration of Independence to the issue of slavery. Additionally, the reader should note a significant shift in the line, "but, Sir, how pitiable…respect to yourselves." Within the passage Banneker uses words to chastise Jefferson for his inability to extend the same liberties that he once fought for and wrote about to a significant portion of the nation's population. His purpose, then, is to ultimately persuade his audience to support his call for freedom and equality, not only because they are the logical conclusions based on the audience's own prior declarations, but also because freedom and equality are granted by the "Creator."

Finally, given this interplay between the persona, audience, and purpose, you should arrive at the passage's central **argument**, which, in essence, provides the reason for the purpose as stated above. Benjamin Banneker argues to Thomas Jefferson that any restriction of freedom and liberty goes against, not only the founding ideals of the nation but also the principles and values of the Creator of mankind. Therefore, because the audience, Thomas Jefferson, championed liberty and freedom during the period of America's fight for independence from England, he should do the same for Banneker's "brethen."

Examining a Passage's Structure:

When examining a passage from the AP® English Language and Composition Exam, it is also important to consider how the passage's argument or central idea is organized and presented to the audience. In other words: How does the passage's **structure** help to develop the logic of its argument?

A strategy that is particularly useful is to annotate the central idea of each paragraph in the margin. This serves two purposes: it allows you quick access back into the text when responding to the multiple-choice questions—as your annotations function as an index of passage's ideas—and it allows you to see a rough outline of the author's argument, helping to illuminate the logic and organization of the author as well as the relationship between the various "parts" or "paragraphs" of the author's argument. This concept of "rhetorical parts" will be examined in more depth when we examine the analysis writing prompt.

With regard to structure, you will, in general, see variations of the following stem questions on the AP® English Language and Composition Exam:

In relation to the first sentence (or paragraph), the second sentence (or paragraph) serves to

In relation to the rest of the passage, the final paragraph best serves to . . .

One purpose of the first paragraph is to

The structure of this passage can best be described as

Let's look again at the Benjamin Banneker letter to Thomas Jefferson. As you re-read the passage, consider the purpose of each paragraph and annotate each purpose in the margins. As we discussed in the previous section of this guide, you should use an infinitive phrase when describing the purpose of each part of the passage.

to recall a time in his life when he experienced oppression and the suspension of liberty

Sir, suffer me to recall to your mind that time, in which the arms and tyranny of the British crown were exerted, with every powerful effort, in order to reduce you to a state of servitude: look back, I entreat you, on the variety of dangers to which you were exposed; reflect on that time, in which every human aid appeared unavailable, and in which even hope and fortitude wore the aspect of inability to the conflict, and you cannot but be led to a serious and grateful sense of your miraculous and providential preservation; you cannot but acknowledge, that the present freedom and tranquility which you enjoy you have mercifully received, and that it is the peculiar blessing of Heaven.

to highlight Jefferson's actions in the face of oppression

to highlight Jefferson's lack of action with regard to this similar form of human oppression

to chastise Jefferson

to provide Jefferson with the advice to "put [his] soul in their souls' stead."

This, Sir, was a time when you clearly saw into the injustice of a state of slavery, and in which you had just apprehensions of the horrors of its condition. It was now that your abhorrence thereof was so excited, that you publicly held forth this true and invaluable doctrine, which is worthy to be recorded and remembered in all succeeding ages: ``We hold these truths to be self-evident, that all men are created equal; that they are endowed by their Creator with certain unalienable rights, and that among these are, life, liberty, and the pursuit of happiness.'' Here was a time, in which your tender feelings for yourselves had engaged you thus to declare, you were then impressed with proper ideas of the great violation of liberty, and the free possession of those blessings, to which you were entitled by nature; but, Sir, how pitiable is it to reflect, that although you were so fully convinced of the benevolence of the Father of Mankind, and of his equal and impartial distribution of these rights and privileges, which he hath conferred upon them, that you should at the same time counteract his mercies, in detaining by fraud and violence so numerous a part of my brethren, under groaning captivity and cruel oppression, that you should at the same time be found guilty of that most criminal act, which you professedly detested in others, with respect to yourselves.

I suppose that your knowledge of the situation of my brethren, is too extensive to need a recital here; neither shall I presume to prescribe methods by which they may be relieved, otherwise than by recommending to you and all others, to wean yourselves from those narrow prejudices which you have imbibed with respect to them, and as Job proposed to his friends, "put your soul in their souls' stead;" thus shall your hearts be enlarged with kindness and benevolence towards them; and thus shall you need neither the direction of myself or others, in what manner to proceed herein.

Hopefully you noticed that Banneker's purpose in the first passage is to ask Thomas Jefferson to recall a time in his life when he experienced oppression and the suspension of liberty. In even simpler terms, the author asks the audience to recall a time in which they, too, were oppressed. Additionally, the author also requests Jefferson acknowledge that freedom is, in fact, "a blessing of Heaven." This is important structurally, because the author establishes his analogy, a comparison that will become fundamental to his argument.

The second paragraph's purpose is similar, but rather than recounting the situation, its purpose is to highlight Jefferson's actions in the face of oppression. Jefferson felt so strongly about liberty and freedom that he embraced the revolution and penned the Declaration of Independent, one of the most important documents in the history of mankind.

You should also note that there is a significant shift in the tone of the work in this paragraph, for once Banneker establishes his analogy and asks Jefferson to consider his actions in the face of such injustice, he transitions to the comparable situation of slavery. So the secondary purpose of this paragraph is to highlight Jefferson's lack of action with regard to this similar form of human oppression, despite his lofty words and actions in the events leading to America's independence. You might also notice that the purpose of this second half of the second paragraph is to chastise Jefferson, as the once polite language incorporated in the first half of the letter gives way to more critical language.

The final paragraph's purpose is to provide Jefferson with the advice to "put [his] soul in their souls' stead." This marks a significant shift from the first paragraph. Rather than the polite, complimentary language used in to remind Jefferson of the colonial oppression and the democratic spirit that inspired the revolution and its corresponding documents, Banneker is both critical of Jefferson's hypocrisy and instrumental in providing him with a path by which he might be apply his democratic ideals to the "cruel oppression" experienced by Banneker's brethren.

The structure of this letter is critical to understanding Banneker's logic. By annotating the text as you read it, you will undoubtedly see the analogy Banneker employs to argue against slavery.

Recognizing Common Rhetorical Strategies

You do not need to be armed with a host of technical terms in order to be successful on the AP® English Language and Composition Exam, although familiarizing yourself with some of the more commonly used terms is essential.

The following terminology is not intended to be exhaustive. It does, however represent those terms that are most frequently used in the multiple-choice section of the AP® English Language and Composition Exam. Your text, *Everyday America*, provides examples and definitions for many of the key terms and rhetorical devices needed to be successful on the AP® Language and Composition exam.

Alliteration
Allusion
Anadiplosis
Analogy
Anaphora
Anecdote
Anthropomorphism
Anticlimax
Antimetabole
Antithesis
Aphorism
Apostrophe
Appositive
Assonance
Asyndeton
Chiasmus
Climax
Consonance
Ellipsis
Epistrophe
Euphemism
Extended Metaphor
Hyperbole

Imagery
Irony
Juxtaposition
Litotes
Malapropism
Metaphor
Metonymy
Onomatopoeia
Oxymoron
Paradox
Parenthesis
Periphrasis
Persona
Personification
Pun
Rhetorical Question
Sarcasm
Satire
Simile
Synecdoche
Theme
Zeugma

There are a number of question stems that you may be asked on the AP® English Language and Composition Exam regarding literary and/or rhetorical devices. Expect to see questions similar to the following:

The sentence in line 57 uses which of the following? (the options will include terms from the previously supplied list)

The speaker's use of rhetorical devices in paragraph 3 include all of the following EXCEPT

The metaphor utilized in line 4 accomplishes all of the following EXCEPT

Lines 3–10 rely primarily on (the options will include terms from the previously supplied list)

Line 56 provides an example of (the options will include terms from the previously supplied list)

Diction and Syntax

The terms **diction** and **syntax** are often misused and misunderstood. They need not be, and the more comfortable you are at analyzing how an author uses language to effectively communicate ideas, the better off you will be when taking the AP® exam.

When we speak of the term **diction**, we are interested in the specific words an author selects in communicating and expressing ideas. Words have meaning, and certain words carry more meaning and richer associations than other words;

so when we speak of diction, we are speaking of both a word's literal meaning—its **denotation**—and its implied meaning—its **connotative** meaning.

Additionally, it is important to consider how specific diction impacts the passage or work as a whole. Often, authors select words for a host of reasons, most notably their impact on the passage's overall tone and their contribution to the development of the speaker's persona. With this in mind, you should conscientiously examine each passage for words that work together to create one or both of these effects.

Again, annotating the text and circling key words is a useful strategy. As you read the selected passages on the AP® English Language and Composition Exam, pay close attention to the words the author selects to communicate ideas. Pay close attention to those specific descriptors that provoke a particular or heightened response from their audience, and consider how an author's selection of nouns and verbs helps contribute to the effectiveness of the passage. You should also consider circling words with which you are not familiar, as the College Board often designs questions to test your ability to define difficult or uncommon words by the context in which they appear.

You will see a number of questions designed to test your understanding of the author's use of diction in a passage. Among the stem questions you will inevitably see are the following:

In line 15, the term "____" is best interpreted to mean

The word "____" (line 15) refers to

In the context of line 15–17, "____" most likely means

A writer's word choice also impacts the **tone** of a passage. You should pay close attention to the way in which the author's diction selection contributes to his or her tone toward the subject matter. You will likely see questions like:

The author's tone, as depicted in the word "____" (line 15) is best described as

While a study of diction examines the connotation and denotation of specific words, **syntax** is the study of the way in which groups of words are assembled together into phrases and/or sentences to convey meaning and, in the case of rhetoric, persuade or appeal to an audience.

Again, the passages the College Board selects for inclusion on the AP® exam are rich and complex passages. However, you don't need to be a lexicographer to identify those parts of a selection that are known for their syntactical merit. Most often, questions regarding syntax revolve around issues of **parallelism**, **repetition**, and **reversals** in grammatical structures (for instance, antimetabole).

Parallelism is a scheme of balance that writers use for emphasis, clarity, or sentence variety. When parallelism is employed by a writer, two or more similar words, phrases, and/or clauses are balanced grammatically. One example of parallelism occurs in Abraham Lincoln's memorable Gettysburg Address. He states:

"Four score and seven years ago our fathers brought forth on this continent a new nation, conceived in liberty, and dedicated to the proposition that all men are created equal."

You will notice in this passage, Lincoln makes use of successive parallel phrases "conceived in liberty" and "dedicated to the proposition that all men are created equal" to emphasize the genesis of the American concept of freedom and equality. Here the syntactical pattern mimics the unity and balance needed to adhere to the ideals set forth by America's Founding Fathers.

In the next passage from the same speech, Lincoln states:

> "Now we are engaged in a great civil war, testing whether that nation, or any nation so conceived and so dedicated, can long endure. We are met on a great battlefield of that war. We have come to dedicate a portion of that field, as a final resting place for those who here gave their lives that that nation might live. It is altogether fitting and proper that we should do this."

This example of parallelism incorporates the repetition of the successive clauses "we are engaged," "we are met," and "we have come to dedicate." **Repetition** refers to words, clauses, or phrases that are used repeatedly for rhetorical effect. It can occur anywhere in the sentence, but often you will see writers repeat key words, clauses, or phrases in successive sentences for rhetorical effect. Such repetition at the beginning of successive clauses is called **anaphora**.

Anaphora is also utilized in the next line of Lincoln's address:

> "But, in a larger sense, we can not dedicate—we can not consecrate—we can not hallow—this ground."

Here Lincoln repeats parallel structures for emphasis and utilizes anaphora to highlight the collective "we" he claims unable to fittingly dedicate, consecrate, or hallow the battlefield.

Finally, you will a notice that Lincoln concludes the Gettysburg Address with successive subordinate clauses, each offset with a dash and beginning with the word "that."

> "It is rather for us to be here dedicated to the great task remaining before us—that from these honored dead we take increased devotion to that cause for which they gave the last full measure of devotion—that we here highly resolve that these dead shall not have died in vain—that this nation, under God, shall have a new birth of freedom—and that government of the people, by the people, for the people, shall not perish from the earth."

Each subordinate clause is parallel in grammatical structure to the other, adding to the rhetorical effect of the passage. You might also note this series of successive subordinate clauses builds to a climax.

Finally, a **reversal** in grammatical structure is, like parallelism, a scheme of balance, in which a syntactical structure is literally reversed for effect. Consider the famous words of John F. Kennedy: "Ask not what your country can do for you—ask what you can do for your country." In this case, the words "country" and "you" reverse positions in each part of Kennedy's memorable line ("country" in the first part is in the subject position of the clause, but shifts in the second part of the sentence to the predicate position, swapping places with the pronoun "you").

There are, of course, other ways in which syntax contributes to the rhetorical effect of a passage. You should also be conscious of clauses or **phrases that interrupt or delay** the information being provided or the action taking place in the sentence. Often this occurs when a phrase or clause is embedded into a sentence between the subject and its verb. This, in effect, changes the emphasis in the sentence, provides additional information, or allows for parenthetical, offhand commentary. You should be cognizant of how writers use such syntactical devices for effect.

Finally, the **rhetorical question** is another frequently used syntactical structure, one that is generally easy to recognize. A rhetorical question appeals to the audience's passions by posing a question in which the answer is already implied. Consider the following example, from Frederick Douglass's "What to the Slave is the Fourth of July?"

> Must I argue the wrongfulness of slavery? Is that a question for republicans? Is it to be settled by the rules of logic and argumentation, as a matter beset with great difficulty, involving a doubtful application of the principle of justice, hard to understand?

Notice that the answers to Douglass's questions are obvious, assumed. Therefore, the author's use of the rhetorical question is for effect only. Be sure to note rhetorical questions when you see them on the multiple-choice section of the AP® English Language and Composition Exam, as the test writers will undoubtedly construct some questions pertaining to their effect.

There are a host of stems used to pose questions about syntax. You should be prepared to see question similar to the following:

> *Which best describes the syntax of line 55–56?*

> *Lines 13–17 rely primarily on . . .* (one or more of your options may include terms such as repetition, rhetorical questions, chiasmus, anaphora, etc.)

> *The effect of the independent clause " . . . . " might best be described as*

> *The stylistic feature most evident throughout the entire passage is the use of . . .* (one or more of your options may include terms such as repetition, series of phrases, rhetorical questions, parallelism, etc.)

Footnotes and Bibliographical Information

A relatively new addition to the multiple-choice section of the AP® English Language and Composition Exam is the inclusion of questions regarding footnotes and bibliographical information. For some, these questions will pose problems, but for most, the four to five questions will be straightforward and relatively easy to respond to. The key, of course, is to read the footnote or bibliographical information carefully.

Often the footnote will reveal additional information to support the main text. This support may come in the form of a definition, parenthetical commentary, or other essential background information. When analyzing its main purpose, be sure to consider the footnote in light of the main text itself. In other words, go back to the original text to review the context of the footnote. This will generally help you to select the appropriate response and help you to identify the main purpose of the footnote itself.

With regard to footnotes, you will likely see questions similar to the following:

The main purpose of the footnote is to . . .

The date referenced in line 3 of the footnote most probably indictes . . .

Some footnotes will include bibliographical information; thus, a rudimentary understanding of the APA and MLA style manuals is important. Consider the following bibliographical entry:

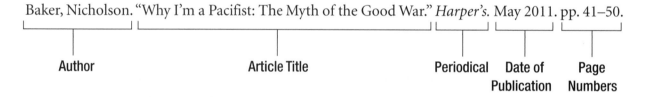

Using the above bibliographical information as a model, you might see questions similar to:

The author cited in line 13 is most likely . . .

The passage is most likely excerpted from . . .

Regardless of the question posed to you, be sure to read the questions carefully and consider all of the possible responses.

Test-Taking Strategies for the Multiple-Choice Section

As stated earlier, there are no short cuts to reading and responding to the questions posed from the selected passages found on the AP® English Language. However, there are some specific strategies you should consider before taking the exam.

Perhaps the most important strategy is to read and annotate the passage carefully. As you prepare for the exam and practice these skills, you will become more adept at predicting specific questions that will be asked of you. Without a doubt, those students who have learned to be active readers—those who **annotate the text and predict potential questions**—perform much better on the

AP® exam than those who simply skim over the passage. The strategies presented in the previous section in this book are sound strategies designed to assist readers in both the comprehension of a text and the rhetorical analysis of it.

In addition to reading and annotating the passage carefully, you should **budget your time judiciously**. Wear a watch and keep an eye on it. Do not spend too much time on any one question or on any one passage. **Circle questions you leave blank**, so you can return to them later, and if you run out of time, **make an educated guess**. There is no penalty for incorrect responses on the AP® exam.

You should quickly **scan the exam to determine how many passages you will need to read and respond to**. Additionally, you should also **consider the time period in which the passages were written**. If you are more comfortable with contemporary passages than with nineteenth-century essays, you may want to read and respond to the contemporary passages before you tackle the more challenging passages. This can help you to budget time.

You should also note that the questions for each passage are arranged sequentially, and not from easiest question to the most difficult. Unless the correct response is obvious to you, you should **return to the targeted point within the text before arriving at a specific answer**.

Finally, you should **relax and move methodically through the exam**. If you have practiced some of the strategies presented in this text and have worked diligently in class in preparation for the exam, you should feel prepared to work confidently and efficiently through the exam questions.

Practice Multiple-Choice Passages and Question Sets

Multiple-Choice: from "If You See Something, Say Something."
**From Thomas Friedman and Michael Mandelbaum—*That Used to Be Us:
How America Fell Behind in the World It Invented*....**

Questions 1–15. Read the following carefully before you choose your answers.

And to maintain American greatness, the right option for us is not to become
more like China. It is to become more like ourselves. Certainly, China has made
extraordinary strides in lifting tens of millions of its people out of poverty and
in modernizing its infrastructure—from convention centers, to highways, to
5   airports, to housing. China's relentless focus on economic development and its
willingness to search the world for the best practices, experiment with them,
and then scale up those that work is truly impressive.

But the Chinese still suffer from large and potentially debilitating problems: a lack of freedom, rampant corruption, horrible pollution, and an educa-
10 tion system that historically has stifled creativity. China does not have better
political or economic systems than the United States. In order to sustain its
remarkable economic progress, we believe, China will ultimately have to adopt
more features of the American system, particularly the political and economic
liberty that are fundamental to our success. China cannot go on relying heavily
15 on its ability to mobilize cheap labor and cheap capital and on copying and
assembling the innovations of others.

Still, right now, we believe that China is getting 90 percent of the potential
benefits from its second-rate political system. It is getting the most out of its
authoritarianism. But here is the shortcoming that Americans should be
20 focused on: We are getting only 50 percent of the potential benefits from our
first-rate system. We are getting so much less than we can, should, and must get
out of our democracy.

In short, our biggest problem is not that we're failing to keep up with
China's best practices but that we've strayed so far from our own best practices.
25 America's future depends not on our adopting features of the Chinese system,
but on our making our own democratic system work with the kind of focus,
moral authority, seriousness, collective action, and stick-to-itiveness that China
has managed to generate by authoritarian means for the last several decades.

In our view, all of the comparisons between China and the United States
30 that you hear around American watercoolers these days aren't about China at all.
They are about us. China is just a mirror. We're really talking about ourselves and
our own loss of self-confidence. We see in the Chinese some character traits that
we once had—that once defined us as a nation—but that we seem to have lost.

Orville Schell heads up the Asia Society's Center on U.S.-China Relations in
35 New York City. He is one of America's most experienced China-watchers. He also

attended the Tianjin conference, and one afternoon, after a particularly powerful presentation there about China's latest economic leap forward, Tom asked Schell why he thought China's rise has come to unnerve and obsess Americans.

"Because we have recently begun to find ourselves so unable to get things done, we tend to look with a certain over-idealistic yearning when it comes to China," Schell answered. "We see what they have done and project onto them something we miss, fearfully miss, in ourselves"—that "can-do, get-it-done, everyone-pull-together, whatever-it-takes" attitude that built our highways and dams and put a man on the moon. "These were hallmarks of our childhood culture," said Schell. "But now we view our country turning into the opposite, even as we see China becoming animated by these same kinds of energies . . . China desperately wants to prove itself to the world, while at the same time America seems to be losing its hunger to demonstrate its excellence." The Chinese are motivated, Schell continued, by a "deep yearning to restore China to greatness, and, sadly, one all too often feels that we are losing that very motor force in America."

The two of us do feel that, but we do not advocate policies and practices to sustain American greatness out of arrogance or a spirit of chauvinism. We do it out of a love for our country and a powerful belief in what a force for good America can be—for its own citizens and for the world—at its best. We are well aware of America's imperfections, past and present. We know that every week in America a politician takes a bribe; someone gets convicted of a crime he or she did not commit; public money gets wasted that should have gone for a new bridge, a new school, or pathbreaking research; many young people drop out of school; young women get pregnant without committed fathers; and people unfairly lose their jobs or their houses. The cynic says, "Look at the gap between our ideals and our reality. Any talk of American greatness is a lie." The partisan says, "Ignore the gap. We're still 'exceptional.'" Our view is that the gaps do matter, and this book will have a lot to say about them. But America is not defined by its gaps. Our greatness as a country—what truly defines us—is and always has been our never-ending effort to close these gaps, our constant struggle to form a more perfect union. The gaps simply show us the work we still have to do.

To repeat: Our problem is not China, and our solution is not China. Our problem is us—what we are doing and not doing, how our political system is functioning and not functioning, which values we are and are not living by. And our solution is us—the people, the society, and the government that we used to be, and can be again.

1. The primary purpose of the first paragraph is to
   (A) chastise American politicians for a failed American economic policy
   (B) applaud the Chinese for their successful economic policies
   (C) urge America politicians to follow the Chinese business model
   (D) establish a contrast that will be further developed in the second paragraph
   (E) formulate a thesis that will be supported throughout the essay

2. The term "debilitating" found in line 8 most nearly means
   (A) depleting
   (B) appalling
   (C) overwhelming
   (D) invigorating
   (E) incapacitating

3. The authors indicate that political and economic liberties are more important to the American model of success than
   I. assembling cheap labor and cheap capital
   II. replicating and mass-producing the innovations of others
   III. permitting social and cultural freedoms

   (A) I only
   (B) II only
   (C) I and II only
   (D) II and III only
   (E) I, II and III

4. The effect of the authors' use of the term "stick-to-itiveness" in paragraph 4 might best be described as
   (A) unsophisticated
   (B) casual
   (C) formal
   (D) vulgar
   (E) pedestrian

5. In light of the paragraph as a whole, the authors' attitude as displayed in the comment, "We are getting only 50 percent of the potential benefits from our first-rate system," (lines 20–21) might best be described as
   (A) ironic
   (B) sardonic
   (C) vitrioloic
   (D) mordant
   (E) incongruous

6. The authors' primary purpose for referencing Orville Shell (paragraphs 6–7) is to
   (A) present a contrasting viewpoint in which to refute
   (B) elaborate upon the metaphor introduced in paragraph 5
   (C) support the premise that America's economic decline in inevitable
   (D) remark on the loss of American self-esteem in the face of Chinese growth
   (E) dispel the myth of American exceptionalism

7. According to lines 39–49, Orville Shell's primary critique of his fellow Americans is that they
   (A) are too idealistic
   (B) do not honor their own past enough
   (C) are too nostalgic and dispirited
   (D) forego innovations for reminiscence
   (E) overlook their own accomplishments

8. The reference "motor force" in line 51 most likely refers to the
   (A) partisan who argues for American exceptionalism
   (B) industriousness and diligence of a nation
   (C) Spartan simplicity of the past
   (D) the spirit of chauvinism that sustains greatness
   (E) internal motivations that lead to greatness

9. In the context of the passage, the word "chauvinism" (line 53) most nearly means
   (A) bigotry
   (B) sexism
   (C) Jingoism
   (D) dogmatism
   (E) prejudice

10. Lines 52–68 include all of the following EXCEPT:
    (A) an allusion
    (B) parenthetical commentary
    (C) a catalogue
    (D) a study in contrasting views
    (E) metonymy

11. It can be assumed from the passage that the intended audience is most likely
    (A) supporters of American exceptionalism
    (B) critics of American elitism
    (C) defenders of a hegemonic state
    (D) pragmatists who both love America and acknowledge its flaws
    (E) patriots willing to defend American policies and elitism

12. The stylistic feature most frequently utilized in the final paragraph of the passage is
    (A) parallelism
    (B) chiasmus
    (C) ellipsis
    (D) hyperbole
    (E) litotes

13. The tone of the passage can best be described as
    (A) sardonic and vitriolic
    (B) didactic and cautionary
    (C) nostalgic and pessimistic
    (D) insightful and optimistic
    (E) indifferent and pedantic

14. Which of the following lines best identifies the central message of the work as a whole?
    (A) Paragraph 2 "China does not have better political. . . . United States."
    (B) Paragraph 3 "We are getting only 50%. . . . first rate system."
    (C) Paragraph 5 "We see in the Chinese some. . . . that we seem to have lost."
    (D) Paragraph 7 "China desperately want to prove . . . demonstrate its excellence."
    (E) Paragraph 8 "But American is not defined by its gaps. . . . we still have work to do."

15. The passage as a whole is most likely excerpted from
    (A) an introduction to a larger analysis of American poitical and economic policies
    (B) a political treatise on American economic policy
    (C) the conclusion to a modern historical textbook documenting current economic issues
    (D) a government document written for congressional review
    (E) a grant designed to fund a non-governmental economic think-tank

Multiple Choice: from William Faulkner's Nobel Prize Speech

Questions 1–15. Read the following carefully before you choose your answers.

Ladies and gentlemen,

I feel that this award was not made to me as a man, but to my work—a life's work in the agony and sweat of the human spirit, not for glory and least of all for profit, but to create out of the materials of the human spirit something which did not exist before.

5 So this award is only mine in trust. It will not be difficult to find a dedication for the money part of it commensurate with the purpose and significance of its origin. But I would like to do the same with the acclaim too, by using this moment as a pinnacle from which I might be listened to by the young men and women already dedicated to the same anguish and travail, among whom is already that one who will some day stand

10 here where I am standing.

Our tragedy today is a general and universal physical fear so long sustained by now that we can even bear it. There are no longer problems of the spirit. There is only the question: When will I be blown up? Because of this, the young man or woman writing today has forgotten the problems of the human heart in conflict with itself which alone

15 can make good writing because only that is worth writing about, worth the agony and the sweat.

He must learn them again. He must teach himself that the basest of all things is to be afraid; and, teaching himself that, forget it forever, leaving no room in his workshop for anything but the old verities and truths of the heart, the old universal truths lacking

20 which any story is ephemeral and doomed—love and honor and pity and pride and compassion and sacrifice. Until he does so, he labors under a curse. He writes not of love but of lust, of defeats in which nobody loses anything of value, of victories without hope and, worst of all, without pity or compassion. His griefs grieve on no universal bones, leaving no scars. He writes not of the heart but of the glands.

25 Until he relearns these things, he will write as though he stood among and watched the end of man. I decline to accept the end of man. It is easy enough to say that man is immortal simply because he will endure: that when the last dingdong of doom has clanged and faded from the last worthless rock hanging tideless in the last red and dying evening, that even then there will still be one more sound: that of his puny

30 inexhaustible voice, still talking.

I refuse to accept this. I believe that man will not merely endure: he will prevail. He is immortal, not because he alone among creatures has an inexhaustible voice, but because he has a soul, a spirit capable of compassion and sacrifice and endurance. The poet's, the writer's, duty is to write about these things. It is his privilege to help man

35 endure by lifting his heart, by reminding him of the courage and honor and hope and pride and compassion and pity and sacrifice which have been the glory of his past. The poet's voice need not merely be the record of man, it can be one of the props, the pillars to help him endure and prevail.

1. The opening lines of the speech help to establish the speaker's
   (A) gratitude
   (B) consternation
   (C) pride
   (D) appeals to authority
   (E) humility

2. One of the speaker's strategies in the first paragraph is to
   (A) recognize the audience for the award
   (B) distinguish the speaker's work from the speaker himself
   (C) flatter those who have offered the speaker acclaim
   (D) moralize about humility
   (E) promote an appreciation for the speaker's publications

3. In line 5, the word "trust" most nearly means
   (A) to rely on the speaker's integrity
   (B) to confide in the speaker
   (C) to place into the care of the speaker
   (D) to trust in the speaker in the future
   (E) to confide in the speaker

4. All of the following rhetorical strategies are employed in the first paragraph EXCEPT
   (A) metaphor
   (B) appositive phrases
   (C) simple sentence
   (D) oxymoron
   (E) personification

5. The question, "When will I be blown up?" (line 13) is most like a reference to
   (A) a work of fiction
   (B) a biblical allusion
   (C) a historical conflict
   (D) a universal question
   (E) a previous speech

6. According to the speaker, contemporary writers have the following problems
   I. the preoccupation with "a general and universal physical fear"
   II. a self-absorbed and self-centered approach to examining life
   III. failure to acknowledge and write about the problems of "the human heart in conflict with itself"

   (A) I only
   (B) II only
   (C) III only
   (D) I and II only
   (E) I, II and III

7. The metaphor of the "workshop" (line 18) accomplishes which of the following?
   (A) It establishes writing as a craft.
   (B) It emphasizes the travails of a writer's life.
   (C) It implies that a myriad of tools are needed to be a successful writer.
   (D) It underscores the speaker's humility.
   (E) It elaborates upon the economic possibilities of writing.

8. The speaker's attitude toward the state of contemporary writing, as referenced in lines 21–24 (He writes not of love . . . but of the glands), can best be described as
   (A) serious and disapproving
   (B) droll and coarse
   (C) apprehensive and foreboding
   (D) didactic and self-aggrandizing
   (E) resigned and somber

9. The speaker's use of the term "glands" (line 24) helps to complete a motif initiated in which of the following lines?
   (A) "the basest of all things" (line 17)
   (B) "the old universal truths" (line 19)
   (C) "he labors under a curse" (line 21)
   (D) "he writes not of love but of lust" (lines 21–22)
   (E) "His griefs grieve on no universal bones" (lines 23–24)

10. The fourth paragraph serves to
    (A) present a contemporary's point of view
    (B) provide a transition
    (C) elaborate on appoint made in the third paragraph
    (D) provide specific examples
    (E) issue a challenge to the audience

11. Which literary device is used in the phrase "ding-dong of doom"?
    (A) metaphor
    (B) assonance
    (C) hyperbole
    (D) alliteration
    (E) personification

12. In lines 34–36 (It is his privilege . . . of his past) the repetition of the conjunction "and" serves to
    (A) present a list of traits from the least to the most important
    (B) emphasize the importance of each individual trait
    (C) create a sense of fluidity through repetition
    (D) chastise the collection of traits individually
    (E) highlight the contradictory language of the human heart

13. The speaker believes that the role of the writer is to
    (A) support and help bring about man's improvement
    (B) record the accomplishments and shortcomings of man
    (C) entertain and provide diversions from the fears of the time
    (D) provide alternate viewpoints for contemporary issues
    (E) help man explore and better understand his carnal nature

14. Given the context of the speech as a whole, the reader can infer its intended audience is
    (A) the panel that gave the speaker the Nobel Prize
    (B) the group of people assembled at the Nobel Prize banquet
    (C) world leaders responsible for the Cold War
    (D) the future recipients of the Nobel Prize for Literature
    (E) popular writers of the time period

15. The purpose of the speech includes all of the following EXCEPT:
    (A) to inspire faith in the human heart
    (B) to challenge conventional writers
    (C) to encourage young and future writers
    (D) to elevate the role of fiction
    (E) to share the award with colleagues and the Nobel committee

Multiple Choice: from Alexander Pope's Essay on Criticism

Questions 1–15. Read the following carefully before you choose your answers.

But most by Numbers judge a Poet's Song,
And smooth or rough, with them, is right or wrong;
In the bright Muse tho' thousand Charms conspire,
Her Voice is all these tuneful Fools admire,
5   Who haunt Parnassus but to please their Ear,
Not mend their Minds; as some to Church repair,
Not for the Doctrine, but the Musick there.
These Equal Syllables alone require,
Tho' oft the Ear the open Vowels tire,
10   While Expletives their feeble Aid do join,
And ten low Words oft creep in one dull Line,
While they ring round the same unvary'd Chimes,
With sure Returns of still expected Rhymes.
Where-e'er you find the cooling Western Breeze,
15   In the next Line, it whispers thro' the Trees;
If Chrystal Streams with pleasing Murmurs creep,
The Reader's threaten'd (not in vain) with Sleep.
Then, at the last, and only Couplet fraught
With some unmeaning Thing they call a Thought,
20   A needless Alexandrine ends the Song,
that like a wounded Snake, drags its slow length along.
Leave such to tune their own dull Rhimes, and know
What's roundly smooth, or languishingly slow;
And praise the Easie Vigor of a Line,
25   Where Denham's Strength, and Waller's Sweetness join.
True Ease in Writing comes from Art, not Chance,
As those move easiest who have learn'd to dance,
'Tis not enough no Harshness gives Offence,
The Sound must seem an Eccho to the Sense.
30   Soft is the Strain when Zephyr gently blows,
And the smooth Stream in smoother Numbers flows;
But when loud Surges lash the sounding Shore,
The hoarse, rough Verse shou'd like the Torrent roar.
When Ajax strives, some Rocks' vast Weight to throw,
35   The Line too labours, and the Words move slow;
Not so, when swift Camilla scours the Plain,
Flies o'er th'unbending Corn, and skims along the Main.
Hear how Timotheus' vary'd Lays surprize,
And bid Alternate Passions fall and rise!
40   While, at each Change, the Son of Lybian Jove

Now burns with Glory, and then melts with Love;
Now his fierce Eyes with sparkling Fury glow;
Now Sighs steal out, and Tears begin to flow:
Persians and Greeks like Turns of Nature found,
45 And the World's Victor stood subdu'd by Sound!
The Pow'rs of Musick all our Hearts allow;
And what Timotheus was, is Dryden now.

---

[1] Parnassus. Mount Parnassus is a mountain in central Greece near Delphi. In Greek mythology, this mountain was sacred to Apollo and the home of the Muses.

[2] Denham and Waller. Sir John Denham was an English poet who was also an actively involved Royalist during the English Civil War of the 1640's. Edmund Waller was an orator and poet who was known for writing poems praising the heads of both sides during the English Civil War.

[3] Camilla. A figure in Roman mythology, Camilla was the servant of Diana and a fierce warrior in her own right. Virgil wrote:

> Last, from the Volscians fair Camilla came,
> And led her warlike troops, a warrior dame;
> Unbred to spinning, in the loom unskill'd,
> She chose the nobler Pallas of the field.
> Mix'd with the first, the fierce virago fought,
> Sustain'd the toils of arms, the danger sought,
> Outstripp'd the winds in speed upon the plain,
> Flew o'er the fields, nor hurt the bearded grain:
> She swept the seas, and, as she skimm'd along,
> Her flying feet unbath'd on billows hung.
> Men, boys, and women, stupid with surprise,
> Where'er she passes, fix their wond'ring eyes:
> Longing they look, and, gaping at the sight,
> Devour her o'er and o'er with vast delight;
> Her purple habit sits with such a grace
> On her smooth shoulders, and so suits her face;
> Her head with ringlets of her hair is crown'd,
> And in a golden caul the curls are bound.
> She shakes her myrtle jav'lin; and, behind,
> Her Lycian quiver dances in the wind.

The Internet Classics Archive. "The Aeneid by Virgil." *The Internet Classics Archive | The Aeneid by Virgil*. N.p., n.d. Web. 11 Nov. 2012.

1. The tuneful "Fools" in line 4 refers to
   I. Those who judge a work of literary merit on its metrical form
   II. Those who prefer a work's style as opposed to its message
   III. Those who wish to indoctrinate others

   (A) I only
   (B) II only
   (C) III only
   (D) I and II
   (E) I, II and III

2. Pope's message in line 11 is reinforced by his use of
   (A) monosyllabic diction
   (B) rhyme and meter
   (C) onomatopoeia
   (D) alliteration
   (E) assonance

3. The primary effect of Pope's parenthetical comment "(not in vain)" is
   (A) to mock by example an informal style
   (B) to lambast the reader's attention span
   (C) to criticize trite and clichéd writing
   (D) to inject humor into the passage
   (E) to comment on the vanity of self-effusive literature

4. Lines 14–17 best contrast
   (A) Lines 8–13
   (B) Lines 18–21
   (C) Lines 22–25
   (D) Lines 30–33
   (E) Lines 40–45

5. The term "Alexandrine" in line 20 most nearly means
   (A) a line of poetry embedded with a caesura
   (B) an homage to Alexander the Great
   (C) a line written in iambic pentameter
   (D) a line utilizing internal rhyme
   (E) a line with twelve syllables

6. A major shift in Pope's essay occurs in which of the following line numbers?
   (A) Line 22
   (B) Line 24
   (C) Line 26
   (D) Line 40
   (E) Line 45

7. In line 34, the effect of Ajax's efforts at throwing "some rocks' vast weight" is enhanced by the line's
   (A) alliteration
   (B) consonance
   (C) imagery
   (D) meter
   (E) assonance

8. The speaker's attitude toward Timotheus in lines 38–47 can best be described as
   (A) admiration
   (B) jealousy
   (C) disdain
   (D) veneration
   (E) critical

9. The tone of the passage might best be described as
   (A) caustic and arrogant
   (B) haughty and ironic
   (C) whimsical and playful
   (D) wrathful and indignant
   (E) admiring and aspiring

10. The author's purpose is all of the following EXCEPT
    (A) to elevate writers like Dryden
    (B) to lambaste cultural critics
    (C) to mock popular literature
    (D) to provide examples of literary devices at work
    (E) to celebrate the diversity of writing styles

11. The main purpose of the footnotes is to
    (A) provide context for Pope's prose
    (B) contrast Pope's view point with that of Waller and Denham
    (C) highlight Pope's education
    (D) explain Pope's position on the politics of his time
    (E) expose Pope's veneration for Greek and Roman mythology

12. The explanations of Waller's and Denham's roles during the English Civil War is most likely included in the footnote in order to
    (A) create a contrast between the two
    (B) establish their relationship with Pope
    (C) emphasize their importance to seventeenth-century literature
    (D) explain Pope's choice of the words "strength" and "sweetness"
    (E) connect Pope to the politics of his time

13. The footnotes assume that contextual evidence is needed for all of the following EXCEPT
    (A) Greek mythology
    (B) the English Civil War
    (C) topographical terminology
    (D) Roman mythology
    (E) oratorical strategies

14. The abbreviation n.p. most likely stands for
    (A) not published
    (B) not public domain
    (C) no date of publication
    (D) no person or author known
    (E) no publisher's name provided

15. In the bibliographical information following the footnote on Camilla, the date, November 11, 2012, refers to
    (A) the original publication date
    (B) the date the cite was last updated
    (C) the date the cite was accessed
    (D) the date of the most recent translation
    (E) the date the publication was made available on the Internet

Multiple Choice: from Robert F. Kennedy—April 4, 1968

Questions 1–15. Read the following carefully before you choose your answers.

Ladies and Gentlemen—I'm only going to talk to you just for a minute or so this evening. Because . . .

I have some very sad news for all of you, and I think sad news for all of our fellow citizens, and people who love peace all over the world, and that is that Martin Luther
5   King was shot and was killed tonight in Memphis, Tennessee.

Martin Luther King dedicated his life to love and to justice between fellow human beings. He died in the cause of that effort. In this difficult day, in this difficult time for the United States, it's perhaps well to ask what kind of a nation we are and what direction we want to move in.
10 For those of you who are black—considering the evidence evidently is that there were white people who were responsible—you can be filled with bitterness, and with hatred, and a desire for revenge.

We can move in that direction as a country, in greater polarization—black people amongst blacks, and white amongst whites, filled with hatred toward one another. Or
15 we can make an effort, as Martin Luther King did, to understand and to comprehend, and replace that violence, that stain of bloodshed that has spread across our land, with an effort to understand, compassion and love.

For those of you who are black and are tempted to be filled with hatred and mistrust of the injustice of such an act, against all white people, I would only say that
20 I can also feel in my own heart the same kind of feeling. I had a member of my family killed, but he was killed by a white man.

But we have to make an effort in the United States, we have to make an effort to understand, to get beyond these rather difficult times.

My favorite poet was Aeschylus. He once wrote: "Even in our sleep, pain which
25 cannot forget falls drop by drop upon the heart, until, in our own despair, against our will, comes wisdom through the awful grace of God."

What we need in the United States is not division; what we need in the United States is not hatred; what we need in the United States is not violence and lawlessness, but is love and wisdom, and compassion toward one another, and a feeling of justice toward those
30 who still suffer within our country, whether they be white or whether they be black.

So I ask you tonight to return home, to say a prayer for the family of Martin Luther King, yeah that's true, but more importantly to say a prayer for our own country, which all of us love—a prayer for understanding and that compassion of which I spoke. We can do well in this country. We will have difficult times. We've had difficult times
35 in the past. And we will have difficult times in the future. It is not the end of violence; it is not the end of lawlessness; and it's not the end of disorder.

But the vast majority of white people and the vast majority of black people in this country want to live together, want to improve the quality of our life, and want justice for all human beings that abide in our land.
40 Let us dedicate ourselves to what the Greeks wrote so many years ago: to tame the savageness of man and make gentle the life of this world.

Let us dedicate ourselves to that, and say a prayer for our country and for our people. Thank you very much.

1. The intended audience of this speech is most likely
   (A) the family of Martin Luther King
   (B) the American people
   (C) polarized people
   (D) potential rioters
   (E) citizens of the world

2. The speaker's attitude towards the death of Martin Luther King, Jr. might best be described as
   (A) regretful and vengeful
   (B) erudite and aloof
   (C) matter-of-fact and solemn
   (D) folksy and contrived
   (E) reverent and somber

3. The purpose of paragraphs 4 and 5 (lines 10–17), in light of the information conveyed in the speech's first three paragraphs, might best be described as
   (A) to examine alternate approaches to the current problem
   (B) to offer comfort in a time of pain
   (C) to examine the polarized nature of the nation
   (D) to question the existence of violence in the nation
   (E) to challenge disparate groups to love one another

4. The phrase, "the stain of bloodshed that has spread across our land" (line 16) is an example of
   (A) an appositive phrase
   (B) an independent clause
   (C) a gerund phrase
   (D) a participial phrase
   (E) parenthetical commentary

5. The speaker's strategy, presented in lines 19–21 ("I would only say that . . . killed by a white man"), is a(n)
   (A) persuasive appeal to the speaker's character
   (B) emotional appeal
   (C) appeal to reason
   (D) example of deductive reasoning
   (E) appeal to fear

6. The purpose of quoting the Greek poet, Aeschylus, in lines 24–26 ("even in our sleep . . . grace of God") is to
   (A) emphasize the educated nature of the speaker
   (B) appeal to the humanist education of the audience
   (C) refer to a literary and historical authority figure
   (D) develop a didactic attitude
   (E) offer a diversion in thought

7. The word "awful" in line 26 most nearly means
   (A) atrocious
   (B) alarming
   (C) awe-inspiring
   (D) appalling
   (E) abysmal

8. The primary rhetorical strategy utilized in lines 27–30 is
   (A) personification
   (B) chiasmus
   (C) zeugma
   (D) anaphora
   (E) periphrasis

9. The effect of the speaker's use of parallel structures in lines 34–36 is to
    I. create a sense of collective identity among the audience
    II. emphasize the troubles of the past in light of a hopeful future
    III. highlight the continual tide of troubles faced by man

    (A) I only
    (B) II only
    (C) III only
    (D) I and II only
    (E) I and III only

10. In light of the tenth paragraph, the purpose of the eleventh paragraph (lines 37–39) is
    (A) to create a sense of unity
    (B) to shame those who do not wish for peace
    (C) to highlight positive human qualities and aspirations
    (D) to condone pacifism as an alternative to violence
    (E) to examine and refute an opposing viewpoint

11. The goal of the speaker's use of the first person plural pronoun "us" in lines 40 and 42 is to
    (A) create an adversarial relationship with his audience
    (B) welcome the audience to join him in his crusade
    (C) assert his authority subtly over his audience
    (D) unify his audience in a pursuit of peace
    (E) allow for a moment of collective contemplation on the future

12. The tone of the speech as a whole might best be described as
    (A) inauthentic
    (B) disingenuous
    (C) buoyant
    (D) contrite
    (E) hopeful

13. The speech utilizes all of the following rhetorical strategies EXCEPT
    (A) parallelism
    (B) allusion
    (C) repetition
    (D) imagery
    (E) chiasmus

14. The overall purpose of the speech as a whole is to
    (A) elevate the universal and time-honored desire to seek out the best in man
    (B) assuage the guilt felt by white Americans for the death of Martin Luther King
    (C) augment polarization among the populace
    (D) use the death as a platform for self-aggrandizement
    (E) politicize the death of Martin Luther King

15. The speaker most likely is a
    (A) newscaster
    (B) statesman
    (C) spokesman for Martin Luther King
    (D) historical scholar
    (E) police official

Multiple Choice: Mary Antin, from *The Promise of Free Education*

Questions 1–15. Read the following carefully before you choose your answers.

Education was free. That subject my father had written about repeatedly, as comprising his chief hope for us children, the essence of American opportunity, the treasure that no thief could touch, not even misfortune or poverty. It was the one thing that he was able to promise us when he sent for us; surer, safer than
5 bread or shelter. On our second day I was thrilled with the realization of what this freedom of education meant. A little girl from across the alley came and offered to conduct us to school. My father was out, but we five between us had a few words of English by this time. We knew the word school. We understood. This child, who had never seen us till yesterday, who could not pronounce our
10 names, who was not much better dressed than we, was able to offer us the freedom of the schools of Boston! No application made, no questions asked, no examinations, rulings, exclusions; no machinations, no fees. The doors stood open for every one of us. The smallest child could show us the way.

   This incident impressed me more than anything I had heard in advance of
15 the freedom of education in America. It was a concrete proof—almost the thing itself. One had to experience it to understand it.

   It was a great disappointment to be told by my father that we were not to enter upon our school career at once. It was too near the end of the term, he said, and we were going to move to Crescent Beach in a week or so. We had to wait
20 until the opening of the schools in September. What a loss of precious time—from May till September! . . .

   The apex of my civic pride and personal contentment was reached on the bright September morning when I entered the public school. That day I must always remember, even if I live to be so old that I cannot tell my name. To
25 most people their first day at school is a memorable occasion. In my case the importance of the day was a hundred times magnified, on account of the years I had waited, the road I had come, and the conscious ambitions I entertained.

   I am wearily aware that I am speaking in extreme figures, in superlatives. I wish I knew some other way to render the mental life of the immigrant child
30 of reasoning age. I may have been ever so much an exception in acuteness of observation, powers of comparison, and abnormal self-consciousness; none the less were my thoughts and conduct typical of the attitude of the intelligent immigrant child toward American institutions. And what the child thinks and feels is a reflection of the hopes, desires, and purposes of the parents who
35 brought him overseas, no matter how precocious and independent the child may be. Your immigrant inspectors will tell you what poverty the foreigner brings in his baggage, what want in his pockets. Let the overgrown boy of twelve, reverently drawing his letters in the baby class, testify to the noble dreams and high ideals that may be hidden beneath the greasy caftan of the
40 immigrant. Speaking for the Jews, at least, I know I am safe in inviting such an investigation. . . .

   The two of us stood a moment in the doorway of the tenement house on Arlington Street, that wonderful September morning when I first went to

school. It was I that ran away, on winged feet of joy and expectation; it was she
45 whose feet were bound in the treadmill of daily toil. And I was so blind that I
did not see that the glory lay on her, and not on me.

Father himself conducted us to school. He would not have delegated that
mission to the President of the United States. He had awaited the day with
impatience equal to mine, and the visions he saw as he hurried us over the sun-
50 flecked pavements transcended all my dreams. Almost his first act on landing
on American soil, three years before, had been his application for naturalization.
He had taken the remaining steps in the process with eager promptness, and at
the earliest moment allowed by the law, he became a citizen of the United
States. It is true that he had left home in search of bread for his hungry family,
55 but he went blessing the necessity that drove him to America. The boasted
freedom of the New World meant to him far more than the right to reside, travel,
and work wherever he pleased; it meant the freedom to speak his thoughts, to
throw off the shackles of superstition, to test his own fate, unhindered by
political or religious tyranny. He was only a young man when he landed—
60 thirty-two; and most of his life he had been held in leading-strings. He was
hungry for his untasted manhood.

1. The author is most likely
   (A) reminiscing about the past
   (B) commenting on the inequity of
       immigrant education
   (C) criticizing opportunity for immigrants
       in America
   (D) reflecting on the role of fatherhood
   (E) examining the values of friendship

2. Which syntactical choice is repeated in the
   first paragraph of the passage?
   (A) anaphora
   (B) chiasmus
   (C) telegraphic sentence
   (D) zeugma
   (E) synecdoche

3. The phrase "the treasure that no thief could
   touch" (line 3) is an example of a(n)
   (A) anaphora
   (B) allusion
   (C) apostrophe
   (D) hyperbole
   (E) appositive

4. Lines 11 and 12 ("no application made . . .
   no fees") emphasizes
   (A) the ease of joining the American
       education system
   (B) the fact that going to school did not cost
       money
   (C) the tribulations experienced by an
       immigrant child
   (D) the freedom of American institutions
   (E) the fact that illiteracy did not bar the
       speaker from enrolling

5. The purpose of the third paragraph, in light
   of the second, is to
   (A) emphasize the desires of the speaker
   (B) disparage the roll of parents
   (C) explain the speaker's change of location
   (D) highlight the nomadic nature of early
       immigrants
   (E) criticize the exclusive nature of the
       American education system

6. Paragraph 4 uses all of the following rhetorical devices EXCEPT
   (A) hyperbole
   (B) parallel construction
   (C) antithesis
   (D) imagery
   (E) metaphor

7. Lines 37–38, "the overgrown boy of twelve, reverently drawing his letters in the baby class" is an example of
   (A) metaphor
   (B) hyperbole
   (C) imagery
   (D) alliteration
   (E) personification

8. The word "caftan" (line 39) most nearly means
   (A) persona
   (B) expression
   (C) apparel
   (D) demeanor
   (E) appearance

9. The speaker's attitude towards her father might best described as
   (A) reverent and awe-struck
   (B) disparaging and irreverent
   (C) respectful and grateful
   (D) angry and resentful
   (E) proud and deferential

10. "Leading strings" in line 60 most nearly means
    (A) restraints
    (B) high regards
    (C) captivity
    (D) suspension
    (E) contempt

11. "He was hungry for his untasted manhood" (lines 60–61) reveals
    (A) his desire for independence
    (B) his quest to seek a spouse
    (C) his attempt to assert his power over his children
    (D) his lack of refinement
    (E) his yearning for social mobility

12. Which of the following devices is used most frequently throughout the passage?
    (A) imagery
    (B) metaphor
    (C) apostrophe
    (D) personification
    (E) cataloging

13. The essence of American opportunity according to the author's father includes which of the following?
    I. the chance to determine one's own destiny
    II. the freedom of speech
    III. the opportunity to accumulate wealth

    (A) I only
    (B) I and II
    (C) I and III
    (D) II and III
    (E) I, II and III

14. What does the author's tone indicate about her attitude towards America?
    (A) she prefers her native homeland
    (B) she reveres democracy but deplores the state of the slums
    (C) she is disappointed by the actual America that contrasts her father's promises
    (D) she celebrates the hope and opportunity represented by American ideals
    (E) she desires to improve upon the basic tenets of American democracy

15. The purpose of the passage as a whole might best be described as an opportunity
    (A) to reminisce about childhood friendships
    (B) to provide a path for success for other immigrants
    (C) to advocate for improvement to American education
    (D) to reflect on the role of parents in shaping one's dreams and aspirations
    (E) to expose the shortcomings of the naturalization process

Answers and Explanations

ANSWERS AND EXPLANATIONS

Multiple-Choice Questions

▌ **1. (D) is correct.** The author in paragraph one examines the relative successes, the "extraordinary strides," made by the Chinese in recent years. The paragraph is, however, followed by "debilitating problems" still present in China today. Thus the first two paragraphs offer two contrasting views of China.

▌ **2. (E) is correct.** To incapacitate is to deprive something of its ability to be effective. Issues like pollution and lack of freedom are issues that thwart the effectiveness of the Chinese political and economic systems.

▌ **3. (C) is correct.** The author explicitly states this point at the end of the second paragraph.

▌ **4. (B) is correct.** The term is highly colloquial and promotes a casual air to the piece, particularly in contrast to the other terms used in the same list.

▌ **5. (A) is correct.** Particularly considering the statistic regarding China "getting 90 percent of the potential benefits from its second-rate political system," the authors' commentary is ironic. One would expect a first-rate political system to receive a higher percentage of benefits.

▌ **6. (B) is correct.** Paragraph 5 introduces the reader to the metaphorical looking glass American's have wistfully been gazing into. Shell's quote extends this metaphor, as he discusses how Americans "view" both themselves and the Chinese.

▌ **7. (C) is correct.** Shell comments on America's nostalgic examination of its past, and also its dispirited nature, specifically when he states America seems "be losing its hunger to demonstrate its excellence.

▌ **8. (E) is correct.** The phrase "motor force" is metaphorical in the sense that it captures America's inner "drive" to be great. It is also refers back to the word "motivation" found at the beginning of the same sentence. Therefore, "motor force" refers to the internal motivations, the driving forces, that inspire a group of people to be great.

▌ **9. (C) is correct.** Jingoism refers to extreme patriotism, and in the context of the passage cited, the authors are referring to the patriotic spirit.

▌ **10. (E) is correct.** Metonymy is a literary device similar to metaphor. There is no example of metonymy present in the passage. The allusion is found in the line "a more perfect union," the parenthetical commentary is offset by the dashes, the catalogue appears when listing American imperfections, and the study in contrasting views appears when examining the partisans and the cynics.

11. (D) is correct. The passage, particularly its use of the second person pronoun "we" and its willingness to examine America's accomplishments as well as its imperfections, suggests that the author and the audience are pragmatic and moderate in their opinions and assertions.

12. (A) is correct. The are a number of parallel constructions in this final paragraph, from the balance established in the first sentence to the string of clauses that follow the dash in the second sentence.

13. (D) is correct. The authors examine the issue of American economic policies in an open-minded manner, providing insight into multiple views held by Americans. They also offer insightful opinion and challenge the accepted opinion of American decline. They are willing to acknowledge American shortcomings, but are optimistic with regard to our future.

14. (E) is correct. The passage as a whole builds to this point. The author believes that America's very history has been defined by its ability to address its gaps. The current economic issue is yet another gap that America will—given its history—address.

15. (A) is correct. The final paragraphs allude to the fact that this passage is an introduction to a much larger work.

Multiple Choice: from William Faulkner's Nobel Prize Speech

ANSWERS AND EXPLANATIONS

Multiple-Choice Questions

▌ **1. (E) is correct.** By focusing on his work as opposed to himself, the speaker expresses humility despite the great honor being bestowed upon him.

▌ **2. (B) is correct.** The first sentence of the speech alludes to this point, with Faulkner, the speaker, asking his audience to acknowledge his work for its ability to explore the human spirit in new and original ways.

▌ **3. (C) is correct.** The term trust, as it is used in this passage, is used in the legal sense. When something is placed in a trust, it is being held in protective custody until its recipient is ready or able to accept possession or ownership of or administer control over it.

▌ **4. (D) is correct.** An oxymoron is an expression with contradictory words. The passage makes use of metaphor (pinnacle), multiple appositive phrases (offset by dashes), a simple sentence, and the personification of the authors "work," but there are no oxymorons.

▌ **5. (C) is correct.** The reference is to the Cold War. During Faulkner's life, the United States and the Soviet Union developed an adversarial relationship that many feared would end in nuclear annihilation.

▌ **6. (E) is correct.** Paragraph 2 asserts that all three of these issues are problems faced by contemporary authors. The third option is the result of the previous two.

▌ **7. (A) is correct.** The workshop is an apt metaphor, as it emphasizes the labor and craftsmanship that go into designing a work of fiction. The speaker in the following sentence even implies that only the basic tools are needed in such a workshop.

▌ **8. (A) is correct.** The entire speech is serious, but in this passage, the speaker condemns popular writers whose focus is self-centered and whose message is transient and trivial. The speaker sees this as a serious problem with writing during his life, and thus condemns those who fail to write about the human condition and the human heart.

▌ **9. (D) is correct.** The term "glands" is designed to contrast with the word "heart." In essence, the speaker is contrasting man's spiritual side with his carnal side. Thus, in this sense, glands completes the motif of carnal lust begun in line 39.

▌ **10. (B) is correct.** In paragraph 4, the speaker begins his transition from discussing the current state of popular fiction to his steadfast championship of those writers like himself who continue to write about the human spirit.

▌ **11. (D) is correct.** Alliteration is the repetition of sounds at the beginning of words, often for emphasis or poetical reasons. Here, the –d sound is repeated.

▌ **12. (B) is correct.** The conscious decision to repeat the conjunction "and" can be used sparingly for emphasis, as the speaker has done in this example. The use of the conjunction asks the audience to consider the independent value of each term.

13. (A) is correct. Lines 37–38 utilize the metaphor of the pillar to accentuate the critical need for writers to act as supports for mankind. The speaker even states that it is not enough for the writer to be a mere recorder of history.

14. (D) is correct. In lines 9–10, the speaker references his intended audience: those who will one day stand where he stands now.

15. (E) is correct. While the speaker takes particular care to be humble, his speech never expresses a sense of particular obligation to fellow colleagues or the Nobel committee.

ANSWERS AND EXPLANATIONS

Multiple-Choice Questions

▌ **1. (D) is correct.** The reference to "Numbers" in line 1 refers to a line's metrical pattern, and intimates the value critics place on the sound of poetry. The reference to "pleas(ing) the ear" rather than "mend(ing) the mind," is a clear comment on the way in which critics value style over substance.

▌ **2. (A) is correct.** Each word in line 11 is monosyllabic ("ten low words").

▌ **3. (D) is correct.** This parenthetical comment interrupts the passage much like an aside. It injects the author's sense of humor into his ridicule of critics and popular literature.

▌ **4. (D) is correct.** Lines 30–33 provide examples of more nuanced and artful personification. These lines are the antithesis of lines 14–17 which demonstrate a trite approach to personification.

▌ **5. (E) is correct.** An Alexandrine is a 12-syllable line. Line 21 provides an example of an Alexandrine.

▌ **6. (C) is correct.** Pope is essentially arguing that excellent writing is an art form practiced by masters; it is not the product of chance.

▌ **7. (B) is correct.** The hard "t" sound created by the phrase "vast weight to throw" mimics the strain of throwing rocks.

▌ **8. (D) is correct.** The Speaker clearly admires Timotheus; however, his admiration also honors the Greek poet's contributions and supreme art, placing him figuratively on a pedestal.

▌ **9. (B) is correct.** Pope's tone is in many ways condescending as he is clearly speaking to an elevated audience. It is also ironic in that he spends much of the passage mocking, by example, trite writing.

▌ **10. (E) is correct.** The author's haughty and ironic tone and opinionated position on what qualifies as good writing suggest that he is critical of most popular writing styles and the critics who heap praise upon it.

▌ **11. (A) is correct.** This contextual information is probably unknown to most contemporary readers of Pope's works.

▌ **12. (D) is correct.** Both were revered writers of their time, but both had unique qualities as writers. Here, Pope is commenting on the combination of both of their skills.

▌ **13. (E) is correct.** While Waller was an orator, the footnote does not discuss oratorical strategies.

▌ **14. (E) is correct.** n.p. stands for no known publisher—this is common for older texts found in the public domain on the Internet.

▌ **15. (C) is correct.** This date referes to the date the researcher accessed the information.

Multiple Choice: from Robert F. Kennedy—April 4, 1968

ANSWERS AND EXPLANATIONS

Multiple-Choice Questions

▌ **1. (B) is correct.** While the speech does contain elements that target specific segments of the American populace, as a whole, its target is the American people.

▌ **2. (E) is correct.** The speaker is certainly saddened by the news of MLK's death, but he is also attuned to the words and life of MLK, and hopes to honor MLK's action in life by encouraging his audience to follow in his footsteps.

▌ **3. (A) is correct.** In these paragraphs, the speaker examines the unique approaches that the audience might take given the circumstance. While they might react with violence, he hopes that they react with a grace reminiscent of MLK's actions and words.

▌ **4. (A) is correct.** The phrase is an appositive phrase intended to provide additional details of description to the noun, "violence."

▌ **5. (B) is correct.** The speaker has also lost a loved one to violence, so this is an example of an emotional appeal. The speaker has established his credibility as a result of his own experience.

▌ **6. (C) is correct.** Making reference to a Greek poet speaks to the time-honored wisdom of the message. Often speakers make a classical reference as a logical appeal to the audience.

▌ **7. (C) is correct.** In this sense, awful means full of awe, in the sense that the creator is grand and all powerful.

▌ **8. (D) is correct.** Anaphora is the repetition of words or phrases at the beginning of successive sentences or clauses. In this case, "What we need." is repeated successfully for rhetorical effect.

▌ **9. (E) is correct.** The use of the first-person plural pronoun, "we" invites a sense of collective identity, while the substance of these lines acknowledges that man has, is, and will continue to face hardship.

▌ **10. (C) is correct.** While paragraph 10 highlights the universal and continual hardships faced by man, the 11th paragraph examines those collective traits that speak to the beauty of man and his aspirations.

▌ **11. (D) is correct.** The first-person pronoun has a unifying effect, in that it unites both the speaker and the audience in a common goal or belief.

▌ **12. (E) is correct.** The conclusion establishes this tone. While the news of MLK's death is negative, the speaker's vision and his hope that his audience will consider the merits of MLK's life's work is one filled with hope.

▌ **13. (E) is correct.** Chiasmus is a reversal in syntactical structure, which is a rhetorical strategy that is not utilized within the passage.

▌ **14. (A) is correct.** The final paragraphs speak to the speaker's ultimate purpose. The reference to the Greeks and the earlier reference to Aeschylus also contribute to a theme that embraces those traits that are the best representations of humanity.

▌ **15. (B) is correct.** The speaker was, in fact, Robert F Kennedy. The language and rhetorical strategies employed throughout are reminiscent of a public servant speaking to a national audience, which would disqualify the other options.

Multiple Choice: Mary Antin, from *The Promise of Free Education*

ANSWERS AND EXPLANATIONS

Multiple-Choice Questions

▌ **1. (A) is correct.** The entire excerpt, being an autobiography, is a nostalgic reminiscence of the past. While it is retold from the eyes of a young person, it is told with the wisdom of an adult.

▌ **2. (C) is correct.** The piece opens with a telegraphic sentence, "education was free," and makes further use of the technique in line 8, "we understood."

▌ **3. (E) is correct.** The phrase is a further elaboration upon the "essence of American opportunity." Therefore it is an appositive phrase.

▌ **4. (D) is correct.** All items in the list provided by the speaker emphasize the way in which the American educational system embraced immigrants with open arms during this time period.

▌ **5. (A) is correct.** This section shows the fact that the speaker is so enthusiastic to begin her education in America, that a mere four months seems like an eternity.

▌ **6. (E) is correct.** While the speaker makes use of hyperbole ("a hundred times magnified", line 26), parallel construction ("years I had waited . . . ambitions I had entertained", lines 26–27), antithesis ("in my case . . ." lines 25–27) and imagery ("bright September morning", line 23), metaphor is not used.

▌ **7. (C) is correct.** The depiction of the immigrant child studiously adhering himself to his studies is clearly imagery.

▌ **8. (C) is correct.** A caftan is a loose garment, rather like a tunic.

▌ **9. (C) is correct.** The speaker indicates that she is grateful for her father's role in forwarding her education, and she clearly respects his own desire to better himself.

▌ **10. (A) is correct.** The reference here most likely refers to reins used to lead a horse or other animals.

▌ **11. (A) is correct.** Despite his age of 32, an age at which one has certainly reached manhood, the father is most interested in experiencing the freedoms that America offers.

▌ **12. (E) is correct.** The author makes exhaustive use of listing and cataloging throughout the entire passage. Her use of cataloging far overshadows her use of imagery.

▌ **13. (B) is correct.** There is no mention of the accumulation of wealth within the entire passage. Opportunity and freedom of speech, however, are often discussed.

▌ **14. (D) is correct.** This is an optimistic reminiscence of the author's childhood, one in which she celebrates the hope and opportunity of America as seen through her eyes and those of her father.

▌ **15. (D) is correct.** The emphasis on the speaker's father and his children clearly identifies the purpose of this passage. Note that the passage both begins and ends with an emphasis on the father.

Section III

Introduction to the AP® English Language and Composition Free-Response Section

Overview

For many students, writing in a timed setting can be a daunting experience. Without the extended time to assess, plan and compose an essay, many students turn to unsubstantiated, pedestrian claims and compose overly-contrived essays. While you certainly want to avoid this approach to the essay section of the AP® English Language and Composition Examination, it is important to understand that the College Board does not expect essays written in a timed setting to be comparable to those written in an untimed setting. In fact, AP® graders are instructed to view each essay as a preliminary or first draft. Thus, a student's essay is not necessarily measured in terms of its exhaustive analysis of a selection's rhetoric or in terms of its flawless command of expression, but instead it is rewarded for what is done well under the constraints of time. This, then, needs to be your focus: You need to be methodical in your approach to responding to each of the three essays, but most importantly you need to hone in on those aspects of each prompt you are most comfortable developing. In other words, less is often more.

The Writing Prompts

The AP® English Language and Composition Examination includes three writing prompts you will respond to in a two-hour time period. You will, however, also be given a 15-minute reading period in which you will be allowed to read the prompts and any supporting documents. As in the case of the multiple-choice section of the exam, careful management of your time will be of great benefit to you. Additionally, there are a number of strategies you should consider when responding to each of the three prompts. These strategies will be explored in more detail in this guide, and you will be given a number of opportunities to respond to sample writing prompts designed to hone these skills. Each of the three writing prompts to which you will be asked to respond are unique and require different approaches.

The synthesis essay will ask you to formulate a position on a contemporary issue. You will be given a number of resources that examine the issue from various perspectives. Your task will be to formulate your position using **at least three** of the resources to defend your position. While it is not necessary that you adhere strictly to either the MLA or APA style, you should demonstrate an understanding of documentation and the ability to give credit to your sources.

The second essay tests your analytical skills. You will be given a selection of non-fiction—a letter, an excerpt from a speech, a historical document, an autobiography, an editorial, etc.—and asked to identify not only its speaker's argument, but also those rhetorical devices that help to shape that argument. Many of the strategies discussed in the multiple-choice section of this guide are applicable when approaching the analysis essay. They will be reviewed and expanded in this section.

The third essay, the argument prompt, tests your ability to apply your own knowledge to a contemporary issue. The argument prompt, in fact, asks you to take a position on a contemporary issue using only your inherent knowledge and argumentative skills to defend your position. You might, in coming up with supporting evidence for your claims, consider your studies, your personal experiences, current events, and other works as support for your essay. This prompt is similar, in many ways, to the synthesis prompt, albeit without the supporting documents that offer multiple perspectives that offer multiple perspectives of the situation.

Time Management

You will be given a total of two hours and fifteen minutes to read, plan and compose each of the three essays. Fifteen minutes are designated as a reading period, a time in which you can read the prompts and any supporting documents and consider your approach to successfully responding to them. This will be discussed in more detail in the next section.

The remaining two hours is time dedicated to responding to the three writing prompts. It is absolutely critical that you budget your time wisely. Bring a watch to gauge your progress on the exam. Often, many students spend too much time on the first two essays and leave too little time for the third. It is essential that you avoid this.

As a rule of thumb, you should dedicate time for planning, organizing, composing and editing each essay. Given the 40-minute time frame granted for each essay, you should plan on dedicating at least 25–30 minutes composing your essay, leaving the ten to fifteen remaining minutes as time to plan and revise the essay. It is important that you leave enough time to identify careless errors in mechanics, grammar, spelling and expression, as they can impact the score you receive.

Finally, while AP® graders do not necessarily award essays higher scores based on essay length, there is a pretty clear correlation that suggests higher scores are typically given to well-developed, well-organized and thorough compositions. Very rarely is a top-tier essay fewer than three pages in length. Excellent essays offer multiple examples and a sustained argument, and this often occurs, quite frankly, in essays that are longer than those that score in the lower tiers.

The Reading Period

You will be given a 15-minute reading period in which to read and annotate the prompts and supporting documents provided by College Board. This 15-minute reading period is a relatively new addition to the AP® exam. It was included to provide students additional time in which to read and analyze the supporting documents incorporated with the synthesis prompt, as the test committee felt that the additional reading necessitated additional time. While this time was added specifically for preparation of the synthesis prompt, you may use this time to read the other two prompts and begin to formulate your approach to each of the three essays. You may not, however, begin composing your essays during the reading period.

One strategy you might find useful is to dedicate more time to the prompt that poses the greatest challenge to you. Even though the synthesis prompt requires that you read multiple documents, often the prompt will allow you to draw upon your inherent knowledge of the subject. If this is the case, you may want to allocate more time during the reading period to preparation for the other two essays. If the analysis passage is one that uses archaic language and formal syntax, it may require more time to analyze. Knowing your strengths and weaknesses and planning accordingly is critical to success on the exam. Again, this is a lesson in time management.

The Synthesis Essay

Introduction
In terms of formulating an argument and composing a persuasive essay, the act of synthesizing ideas requires a writer to consider a number of perspectives on an issue. This act is not unlike composing a research paper, an activity you have undoubtedly completed in your studies in language and rhetoric.

Some students complain that research is tedious and often unoriginal, as the researcher is simply using another researcher's data and opinion in order to support a claim. This is a shortsighted outlook on research. What makes research and the process of synthesizing information interesting is the way in which it is compiled and then presented. The art of research lies not in the simple regurgitation of facts and opinions, but in the artful organization of information, information that is presented in a new and fresh manner.

This is the beauty of the synthesis prompt. You will be introduced to a contemporary issue, one that provokes a variety of opinions and a range of nuanced responses. You will be asked to consider the various viewpoints held by experts or commentators in the field, and then to develop—to synthesize—your own position on that topic.

Approaching the Synthesis Prompt
There are no shortcuts to responding to the synthesis prompt. You must decode the prompt itself, read all of the supporting documents, weigh the validity of the opposing viewpoints, consider the implications of such positions, and develop your own position supported by the resources provided.

With regard the prompt itself, the synthesis prompt is formulaic. The prompt itself is divided into three parts: the directions, an introduction, and the assignment. All three of these components are formulaic. The directions specifically change very little from year to year. The introduction presents a contemporary topic and a current issue associated with that topic. The specific assignment will then ask you to examine a body of evidence—the resources provided by the College Board—and to answer the following question: What do you need to consider before arriving at a position? Over the years, the prompts have continued to use the same language in the assignment section of the prompt, particularly with regard to the phrases "develop a position" and what "issues should be considered."

Reading and Analyzing the Supporting Documents

You will be provided typically with eight sources, lettered alphabetically. These sources are compiled from a variety of mediums. You will likely see excerpts from letters, editorials, governmental or non-profit agencies, online sources such as Web sites and blogs, and more traditional print sources like books and other periodicals. You will also likely find images in the form of charts and graphs or in the form of photographs and political cartoons. These images, themselves, offer insight into the issue, and you should consider the ways in which they can enhance or develop your argument (see below for strategies on interpreting images).

When you examine the provided resources, you will undoubtedly notice that each can be classified. Often two to three sources will advance a particular position on the issue at hand; two to three additional sources will then advance opposing viewpoints. The remaining documents will either be factual in nature, as is the case with charts and graphs, or offer more neutral, impartial positions on the issue. Knowing this, one organizational strategy you should consider is to note at the top of each resource whether it supports a position, opposes it, or remains neutral. Use the symbols +, –, and = respectively to classify each resource.

Additionally, while time is limited and you cannot be expected to thoroughly annotate each resource, you should underline or annotate key words, phrases, quotations, or statistics that help to articulate the specific position of each document. You should be able to internalize each specific position if you are to compose an excellent synthesis response.

Most importantly, you must resist the urge to oversimplify the position developed in each source. Each source offers a unique perspective on the issue, and you must seek to differentiate among the nuanced positions promoted in each source. Certainly, there will be similarities among the resources, but you will be assessed, in part, on your ability to develop a nuanced argument that understands the unique positions of each document.

To help you further elaborate upon these nuances, consider and review the following key terms, concepts frequently taught in rhetoric and composition courses:

1. Claim—What is the claim made by the speaker or author of the document?
2. Support—What specific evidence or data is cited or utilized to support the central claim of the document?
3. Warrant—How is the evidence linked to the claim? What are the pre-existing assumptions or beliefs necessary to link the evidence to the claim?

While time is obviously limited, you should consider these concepts and the accompanying questions carefully when analyzing each document. At the very least, you should internalize your responses to them before composing your essay. Ideally, you will provide at the top of each document short, terse responses to these questions as part of the analysis process. Use the reading period to your advantage.

Analyzing and Interpreting Visuals

Analyzing and interpreting visuals such as political cartoons and photographs are an essential skill in the twenty-first century, as they, too, are a part of the rhetorical landscape. Many students simply pass over the images that accompany the synthesis prompt and, instead, select from the print passages. However, the visuals often offer unique positions and opinions on the issue at hand and should be considered carefully when determining which resources to utilize in your response.

A simple strategy for analyzing an image is to follow this three-step process:

1. Where is your eye first directed when examining the image? In what direction does it move as you consider the entire image?
2. What do you see? What are the various component parts of the image?
3. What is the argument? What is the artist's position on the issue at hand? If the image is a political cartoon, you should identify the punch line.

Consider the following image and practice the above-mentioned strategy:

Image 5.1: "An Old Idea"

Essay Structure and the Opposing Argument

Better essays not only offer a compelling argument and evidence to support a clear position on an issue, but they also consider the opposing arguments and offer up evidence to refute them. This is a standard component to the classical approach to argument. The classical approach is useful in a timed setting, and you might consider its simplicity in promoting your position on the issue at hand.

In the classical argument, a thesis is introduced immediately in the essay's opening paragraph. Keep in mind that many AP® graders read hundreds of essays, often in one sitting. It is often to your advantage if the reader can identify your position quickly and succinctly at the onset of the argument.

After articulating your thesis, you should present the logic of your argument, being sure to develop at least two or three distinct sub-claims to support your thesis. Be sure to cite specific evidence from your sources and write from an authoritative position. Be sure to avoid at all costs, phrases such as "I think" or "I feel" as they diminish your credibility.

After presenting your evidence, acknowledge the opposing arguments and be sure to offer a counterargument to each of them. Many students do not consider counterarguments in responding to the synthesis prompt, but by successfully offering a refutation to the opposing arguments, you demonstrate to your audience that you have considered all of the various opinions on the issue carefully. This is a strategy that helps to develop credibility, a key component to any argumentative essay.

Your conclusion might inspire the audience to take action or to consider ways in which to implement your position.

Citing Your Sources

You are required to utilize and cite **at least three** of the provided resources; however, successful essays often cite more. You can do this in a number of ways, but using the MLA or APA approach to parenthetical citation demonstrates a familiarity with the basic tenets of research and documentation. If you decide to use the MLA approach to citations, simply include the author's (or authors') last name in parenthesis at the end of the sentence containing the cited information. The citation is considered part of the sentence and should be inside the concluding period. If a page number is provided, it should follow the author's name in the parenthesis (i.e. A study showed that 40% of the population agreed with the President's position (Smith 26).

If you decide to use the APA approach to documentation, you should provide the author's name in the signal phrase and then follow the name with the publication date in the parenthesis (i.e. In an editorial printed in the *Washington Post*, Smith (2002) stated. . . .). If you chose not to include the author's name in the signal phrase, you should include it and the date of publication in parenthesis at the end of the clause in which the cited information is referenced.

You may, however, simply refer to the sources by their titles in parenthesis (Source A, Source B, etc.), as is instructed in the test booklet. Regardless of your approach, you must cite at least three sources in responding to the prompt.

Failure to do so will severely impact even the most persuasive and articulate responses. In fact, the scoring rubrics state that an essay that cites fewer than three resources can only score a 4 on the AP® 1–9 scoring scale.

Samples

English Language and Composition
Synthesis Prompt

Sample Question 1
(Suggested time: 40 minutes. This question will count for one-third of your total essay section score.)

The Great Recession that began in 2008 was caused in part by questionable lending practices in the financial markets. As a response to the financial crisis, there arose competing calls: those in support of continued deregulation of the financial markets and those in favor of regulations and more governmental oversight.

Read the following seven sources carefully. Then synthesize the information from at least three of the sources and compose a well-written essay in which you take a position on the role of the government in providing both oversight of the financial market and protection to the American citizens.

Make sure your argument is central to the essay. Be sure to use the sources provided to help elucidate and support your position. While it is not necessary that you use the MLA or APA format in citing your sources, you should clearly identify those sources that you use to help develop and support your opinion. You may identify these sources by referring to them as Source A, B, C, etc., or you may provide identifying information in parenthesis.

Source A (Boxer)
Source B (Carnegie)
Source C (Consumer Financial Protection Bureau)
Source D (HR 4173)
Source E (Bachman)
Source F (Congressional Budget Office)
Source G (Jolliffe)

The following is commentary from Senator Barbara Boxer regarding the banking system.

I think it is important for us to remember the real reasons as to why we are taking up this bill. Even though it is painful to review the dark times of 2008, when our economy and the world economy were really on the brink, I believe it is important for us to do that review.

I asked my staff to put together some of the headlines from those days. We are going to go through a couple of charts and I will read a few of them, because we need to remember what it was like in those dark moments in our history.

Here is a picture of a Wall Street trader and he is under a headline that says "Black Monday." It was at a moment when the first bailout happened. It says, "Bailout Fails, Stock Drop Most In History." Then we look at this one: "Where Do We Go From Here?" "NASDAQ: The Biggest Fall Since Dot.com Crash." "Dow Down 778." "Time" magazine, "Wall Street's Latest Downfall: Madoff Charged With Fraud." "Feds' Rescue Plan: The Bailout To End All Bailouts." "Jobs, Wages, Nowhere Near Rock Bottom Yet." "Credit Crunch Continues As Lending Rates Climb." "U.S. Consumer Sentiment Decreases To A 28–Year Low." "U.S. Loses 533,000 Jobs In The Biggest Drop Since 1974."

That is one chart, and I have one other, just to remind us where we were. San Jose Mercury News: "Foreclosure Wave: San Jose Fights To Protect Neighborhoods." "Carnage Continues: 524,000 Jobs Lost." "Wall Street Employees Set To Get $145 billion." That is in bonuses during all of this. "Economy In Crisis," "Foreclosure," "Lehman Files For Bankruptcy," "Merrill Sold," "AIG Seeks Cash." We know all about that. "What now?" "The Dow Falls 777," "Economy On The Brink." "U.S. Pension Insurer Lost Billions In The Market." "Housing Prices Take Biggest Dive Since 1991." "U.S. Drafts Sweeping Plan To Fight Crisis As Turmoil Worsens In Credit Markets." And here is one: "Full Of Doubts, U.S. Shoppers Cut Spending."

I read these headlines to my colleagues to bring back those dark, dark, dark days and why we are here today trying to make sure it never happens again. If we don't learn from history, we are doomed to repeat it, and we have learned and we are ready to make sure this never happens again.

Those dark times came because we allowed Wall Street to engage in unregulated and unsupervised gambling. I have to say I am an economics major. That goes back quite a bit of time. Many years ago, before any of these kinds of exotic instruments were created, I worked on Wall Street as a stockbroker. I can tell my colleagues that every time the President of the United States would sneeze and the market went down a few points, I worried. I can just imagine how I would have felt if I would have had clients in this kind of situation where there was no control.

A shadow banking system grew up that fueled an unsustainable housing bubble. From 2001 to 2007, the issuance of toxic private mortgage-backed securities increased by over 400 percent. These securities were rated by credit rating agencies—the credit rating agencies that were supposed to be tellers of the truth. They are supposed to say to the consumer, uh-oh—I sound like my grandchild who says uh-oh— that is what they are supposed to say: Don't buy those securities because they are not good. But these credit agencies, rating agencies such as Moody's and Standard & Poor's, frankly, acted as though they were in the pockets of the issuers who paid them. In other words, they gave a good answer. If you wanted to issue securities—I don't care whether it is Goldman or anybody else—you go to these fellows, you pay them, and they tell you something good. What went wrong? That is a disaster. Where is the fiduciary responsibility in any of these relationships?

The following is from Andrew Carnegie's essay "Wealth."

Thus is the problem of rich and poor to be solved. The laws of accumulation will be left free, the laws of distribution free. Individualism will continue, but the millionaire will be but a trustee for the poor, entrusted for a season with a great part of the increased wealth of the community, but administering it for the community far better than it could or would have done for itself. The best minds will thus have reached a stage in the development of the race in which it is clearly seen that there is no mode of disposing of surplus wealth creditable to thoughtful and earnest men into whose hands it flows, save by using it year by year for the general good. This day already dawns. Men may die without incurring the pity of their fellows, still sharers in great business enterprises from which their capital cannot be or has not been withdrawn, and which is left chiefly at death for public uses; yet the day is not far distant when the man who dies leaving behind him millions of available wealth, which was free for him to administer during life, will pass away "unwept, un-honored, and unsung," no matter to what uses he leaves the dross which he cannot take with him. Of such as these the public verdict will then be: " The man who dies thus rich dies disgraced."

Such, in my opinion, is the true gospel concerning wealth, obedience to which is destined some day to solve the problem of the rich and the poor, and to bring "Peace on earth, among men good will."

The following is a press release from a governmental agency.

Consumer Financial Protection Bureau Outlines Bank Supervision Approach
CFPB Will Begin Its Examination Program for Large Banks on July 21
WASHINGTON—The Consumer Financial Protection Bureau (CFPB) today outlined the agency's approach to supervising large depository institutions to ensure compliance with federal consumer financial protection laws—a supervisory process that will begin on July 21, 2011.

"The new consumer agency is here to make sure that markets work for American families, and our bank supervision program is a big part of that," said Elizabeth Warren, Special Advisor to the Secretary of the Treasury on the CFPB. "Starting on July 21, we will be a cop on the beat—examining banks and protecting consumers."

Scope of Bank Supervision Program
Leading into the recent financial crisis, consumer financial protection authorities were spread among seven different federal agencies. The Dodd-Frank Wall Street Reform and Consumer Protection Act (Dodd-Frank Act) streamlined consumer protection oversight authority into the CFPB—promoting greater efficiency and accountability for American consumers.

The consumer agency will conduct examinations to help ensure that consumer financial practices at large banks conform with consumer financial protection legal requirements. The CFPB's bank supervision program will oversee the 111 depository institutions that have total assets over $10 billion. Subsidiaries and all other affiliates of these institutions also fall under the CFPB's authority. These institutions collectively hold more than 80 percent of the banking industry's assets.

Staffing and Training
A diverse and talented team of examiners throughout the country, managed out of satellite offices in Chicago, New York, San Francisco, and Washington, D.C., will form the front line in the CFPB's supervisory efforts. Each of these satellite offices will be the nexus for CFPB supervision in their respective areas of the country. Having examiners and field managers focused on these regions will help ensure that the CFPB understands the business practices and dynamics in different markets throughout the country. The examiners working in those regions will spend much of their time onsite at depository institutions and at other consumer financial services companies.

A large part of the CFPB's supervision staff will be made up of experienced examiners: By the end of July, the CFPB supervision team will include more than 100 staff members transferring directly from the Federal Deposit Insurance Corporation, the Federal Reserve System, the Office of the Comptroller of the Currency, and the Office of Thrift Supervision. The CFPB expects eventually to have several hundred examiners on board, coming from a variety of backgrounds, including state regulatory agencies and industry. Experienced examiners will sharpen their skills in workshops before being deployed, and examiners new to consumer financial protection will receive extensive technical and professional skills training.

Supervision Process

CFPB supervision will be an on-going process of pre-examination scoping and review of information, data analysis, on-site examinations, and regular communication with regulated entities, prudential regulators, and as well as follow-up monitoring. For most depository institutions supervised by the CFPB, periodic examinations will be conducted. For the largest and most complex banks in the country, the agency will implement a year-round supervision program that will be customized to reflect the consumer protection and fair lending risk profile of the organization.

Monitoring will be a constructive process, ensuring that, where required, consumer risks are addressed and compliance programs are strengthened. Analyzing information that is unique to the institution—for example, lending activities, fee structures, and marketing practices—as well as assessing product trends at the market level, will also allow the CFPB to detect and address risks to consumers as they develop. Institutions will generally be advised of upcoming examinations and receive status updates throughout the supervision process.

During an examination, the CFPB will assess each institution's internal ability to detect, prevent, and remedy violations that may harm consumers by reviewing the institution's internal procedures and conducting interviews with personnel. Examiners will look at the products and services the institution offers, with a focus on risk to consumers. The institution's compliance with requirements during the entire life cycle of the product or service will be reviewed, including how a product is developed, marketed, sold and managed. Fair lending reviews will be conducted to detect and address potential discriminatory practices, and, more generally, the institution's policies and practices will be evaluated to ensure compliance with consumer financial protection laws and regulations.

If a company is not fully compliant, the CFPB will seek corrective actions, including strengthening the company's programs and processes to ensure that such violations do not recur and, where appropriate, that remedies are instituted. When necessary examiners will coordinate and work closely with CFPB's enforcement staff to implement appropriate enforcement actions to address harm to consumers.

The following is a government document.

H. R. 4173
One Hundred Eleventh Congress
of the
United States of America

AT THE SECOND SESSION
***Begun and held at the City of Washington on Tuesday,
the fifth day of January, two thousand and ten***

An Act

To promote the financial stability of the United States by improving accountability and transparency in the financial system, to end "too big to fail", to protect the American taxpayer by ending bailouts, to protect consumers from abusive financial services practices, and for other purposes.

Be it enacted by the Senate and House of Representatives of the United States of America in Congress assembled,

SECTION 1. SHORT TITLE; TABLE OF CONTENTS.

(a) SHORT TITLE.—This Act may be cited as the "Dodd-Frank Wall Street Reform and Consumer Protection Act."
(b) TABLE OF CONTENTS.—The table of contents

Source E
Cong. Rec. 19 March 2009: H 3689–3690. PDF.

The following is commentary from Barbara Bachman on taxes and the American economy.

Mr. Speaker, I rise today to talk about America's economy and where Americans are at right now. We have seen a lot of trouble over the last 2 years, and it needn't be that way.

We could turn this American economy around next quarter. We could truly bring hope and change to the American people if we would put into place a positive solution that would give people certainty about where they are going to go in this economy, and we can. We know it's possible. It's really fairly simple.

All we need to do is this: we need to get people investing in the economy, and you do that by making incentives for that. I am a former Federal tax lawyer. I have lived this life, I know how it works.

Right now we have a high rate on our capital gains tax. Unfortunately, the Obama administration is looking at increasing that tax. We need to go just in the opposition direction. We need to cut the investment tax called capital gains down to zero. The best thing we could do is make that tax permanent to the investor community.

Let Americans know, if you take your money, and if you put it at risk opening a business, hiring people for jobs, in the next 4 years your risk will be paid off because you will have a 0 percent interest rate. That's capital gains.

If we would permanently lower the capital gains to zero for 4 years, we would have incredible domestic investment, as well as foreign investment. Even better, we can take the business tax rate—the United States today has the second highest business tax rate in the world, 34 percent.

America is not an attractive place to invest money. We can change that. We can go from 34 percent on our business tax and bring that down to 9 percent, make it permanent.

What are foreign investors looking for? A safe haven for investment. They want to invest in the United States, but we have a very punitive investment climate.

If we would bring down that business tax rate to 9 percent, we would be able to bring foreign money into the United States and invest and create jobs. Rather than seeing jobs flee the United States to other countries, we will see them come right back into the United States.

That's what we need now, more jobs, more stability, more certainty. We have had enough with economic uncertainty from 2008 to the present. Let's change that equation. We can have a positive alternative.

First, zero capital gains. Second, lower the business tax rate to be one of the lowest in the world.

Third, cut every American's tax rate down by at least 5 percent. We can do that, and that will help Americans keep more of their money.

Fourth, we need to kill the death tax once and for all. If even one American pays the death tax, it's immoral. Why in the world should Uncle Sam be able to reach in the coffin after death and still try to pull the wallet out of an American who is deceased? This is immoral. It shouldn't be.

Then, finally, the alternative minimum tax, we should zero out the alternative minimum tax, which is putting a second tax burden on already overtaxed middle-class Americans.

Also, Sarbanes-Oxley, Sarbanes-Oxley has actually chased capital out of New York City over to London. We need to get that investment capital back in the United States.

That's a pretty simple plan. If we would stay here for the rest of the day, and if we would stay here tomorrow, as Members of Congress, we could very quickly and simply pass this commonsense legislation that has worked time and time again.

Don't just take my word for it, a woman from Minnesota—take a look at Harvard. Harvard did a study back in 2002 that examined 18 different world economies, and they showed the same thing. They said, what do you do to make economies work, and what do you do that makes economies not work?

Here is what you do, you lower the wages of government employees, you lower transfer payments, welfare payments, and you lower the tax rates. That's what you do, the study concluded, to make economies revive.

What you don't do is increase government spending. What you don't do is increase taxes.

What we have seen in the last 60 days is what you do to make an economy not work or bring more uncertainty into our economy.

The American people deserve a positive solution, and we have got one. Let's get to work, let's stay here, let's make it happen. Instead, what are we seeing happen? We are seeing more spending and higher taxes.

And what did the Federal Reserve try to do this week? They announced that they are going to do another $1 trillion in purchases. And they just announced today another $300 billion in buying up long-term Treasury securities. They have already lowered the interest rates to zero, so now they want to flood more money into the money supply, but this reduces the value of dollar.

There is so much we can do to change the economy. Let's get busy.

The following is a press release from a government agency.

The Budgetary Impact and Subsidy Costs of the Federal Reserve's Actions During the Financial Crisis

May 24, 2010

The financial system plays a vital role in the U.S. economy. It channels funds from savers to businesses, households, and governments that need money to finance investments and other expenditures, and it provides services that are essential for commercial and financial transactions. When the financial system is functioning smoothly, investors trade securities in liquid markets that provide reliable signals about the values of assets, and loans are readily available to creditworthy borrowers. As the nation's central bank, the Federal Reserve System plays an important role in maintaining the stability and liquidity of the financial system through its conduct of monetary policy and its authority as a supervisor and regulator of banking institutions.

Over the past several years, the nation has experienced its most severe financial crisis since the Great Depression of the 1930s. Unexpected losses on subprime mortgages (loans made to borrowers with poorer-than-average credit) as well as heightened uncertainty about how exposed some financial institutions might be to additional losses led to a sharp decline in the liquidity of some markets and the availability of credit. The contraction in lending became more severe as the turmoil spread beyond the subprime mortgage market, several large financial institutions failed, and the economy weakened. Net lending by the private financial sector fell from more than $3.0 trillion in 2007 to annual rates of about $1.4 trillion in the fourth quarter of 2008 and—$1.8 trillion in the first quarter of 2009.

In response to that contraction, the Federal Reserve undertook a series of extraordinary actions to stabilize financial markets and institutions. It continued to use its traditional monetary policy tools, but in addition, it created a variety of targeted credit programs to help restore liquidity and confidence to the financial sector. Its actions included:

- Expanding lending to depository institutions—that is, to financial institutions, such as commercial banks and savings and loan associations, whose liabilities largely consist of checking and savings accounts and other deposits;
- Creating new lending programs, or "facilities," for nondepository financial institutions and other participants in the financial markets;
- Purchasing mortgage-related securities and medium and long-term securities of the U.S. Treasury in the open market to put downward pressure on medium and long-term interest rates in the mortgage and debt markets; and
- Extending support to financial institutions whose failures policymakers believed could lead to a systemic collapse of financial markets and institutions.

The following is an image taken at the Dewey Square encampment of the Boston Occupy Movement.

English Language and Composition
Synthesis Prompt

Sample Question 2
(Suggested time: 40 minutes. This question will count
for one-third of your total essay section score.)

The Wilderness Preservation Act of 1964 was signed into law by President Johnson to protect tracts of land from development and to preserve them in their natural condition for the American people in perpetuity.

Imagine that a large tract of undeveloped land is being considered for wilderness designation. Carefully read the following 7 sources, including the introductory information for each source. Then synthesize the information from at least three of the sources to help identify the key issues that need to be considered when targeting a specific piece of land for wilderness designation.

Make sure your argument is central to the essay. Be sure to use the sources provided to help elucidate and support your position. While it is not necessary that you use the MLA or APA format in citing your sources, you should clearly identify those sources that you use to help develop and support your opinion. You may identify these sources by referring to the as Source A, B, C, etc., or you may provide identifying information in parenthesis.

Source A (National Park Service)
Source B (Radanovich)
Source C (Burton)
Source D (Muir)
Source E (Callahan)
Source F (State of Wisconsin)
Source G (Bureau of Land Management)

The following is from a federal government website providing answers to frequently asked questions about Wilderness.

What is wilderness?

The Wilderness Act, signed into law in 1964, created the National Wilderness Preservation System and recognized wilderness as "an area where the earth and its community of life are untrammeled by man, where man himself is a visitor who does not remain." The Act further defined wilderness as "an area of undeveloped Federal land retaining its primeval character and influence without permanent improvements or human habitation, which is protected and managed so as to preserve its natural conditions. . . ."

Congress has now designated more than 106 million acres of federal public lands as wilderness: 44 million of these acres are in 47 parks and total 53 percent of National Park System lands. Additional national park areas are managed as "recommended" or "proposed" wilderness until Congress acts on their status.

How is wilderness different from other federal public lands?

Designated wilderness is the highest level of conservation protection for federal lands. Only Congress may designate wilderness or change the status of wilderness areas. Wilderness areas are designated within existing federal public land. Congress has directed four federal land management agencies—U.S. Forest Service, Bureau of Land Management, U.S. Fish and Wildlife Service, and National Park Service—to manage wilderness areas so as to preserve and, where possible, to restore their wilderness character.

The Wilderness Act prohibits permanent roads and commercial enterprises, except commercial services that may provide for recreational or other purposes of the Wilderness Act. Wilderness areas generally do not allow motorized equipment, motor vehicles, mechanical transport, temporary roads, permanent structures or installations (with exceptions in Alaska). Wilderness areas are to be primarily affected by the forces of nature, though the Wilderness Act does acknowledge the need to provide for human health and safety, protect private property, control insect infestations, and fight fires within the area. Wilderness areas are managed under the direction of the Wilderness Act, subsequent legislation (such as the Alaska National Interest Lands Conservation Act), and agency policy.

Is designated wilderness necessary in a national park?

The wild, undeveloped areas of national parks (often called "backcountry") are subject to development, road building, and off-road mechanized vehicular use. National park backcountry is protected only by administrative regulations that agency officials can change. The Wilderness Act protects designated wilderness areas by law "for the permanent good of the whole people." With the Wilderness Act, Congress secures "for the American people of present and future generations the benefits of an enduring resource of wilderness."

What is the significance of wilderness?

Through the Wilderness Act, Congress recognized the intrinsic value of wild lands. Some of the tangible and intangible values mentioned in the Wilderness Act include "solitude or a primitive and unconfined type of recreation," as well as "ecological, geological, or other features of scientific, educational, scenic, or historical value." Wilderness areas provide habitat for wildlife and plants, including endangered and threatened species.

Wilderness protects open space, watersheds, natural soundscapes, diverse ecosystems and biodiversity. The literature of wilderness experience frequently cites the inspirational and spiritual values of wilderness, including opportunities to reflect on the community of life and the human place on Earth. Wilderness provides a sense of wildness, which can be valuable to people whether or not those individuals actually visit wilderness. Just knowing that wilderness exists can produce a sense of curiosity, inspiration, renewal and hope.

How does wilderness designation in a park affect people?

Wilderness areas are places where humility and respect play a role in both individual and management activities. People can recreate in wilderness, though in most places individuals do so without mechanical transport. Visitors may hike, fish, camp, watch wildlife, photograph, or hunt (where legally authorized). Most park visitors will probably never enter into a wilderness area, yet they enjoy wilderness as a scenic backdrop to developed park areas.

Source B
Cong. Rec. 25 March 2009: H3843–H3844. PDF.

The following is commentary from Congressman Radanovich (CA) regarding the Omnibus Public Lands Bill.

Mr. RADANOVICH. Madam Speaker, yesterday I went to the Rules Committee and offered an amendment to the Omnibus Public Lands bill that would have saved 80,000 jobs and over $2.2 billion worth of income in my district by ending the regulatory drought that currently plagues the San Joaquin Valley. Surprisingly, the Rules Committee said ``no" to saving 80,000 jobs despite bipartisan support.

My amendment would have temporarily removed the restrictions the Endangered Species Act places on Federal and State water pumps in the California Bay-Delta, allowing water to be moved from northern and central California to farming families in my district and to millions of urban Californians in the southern portion of the State. Pumping and storing more water is necessary if we want to relieve the devastating drought in California. Yet, the Rules Committee didn't consider the billions of dollars and jobs it would save to be worthwhile.

The way this legislation has been put together and shuttled through Congress is atrocious. The majority has sprinkled a few meritorious provisions in an effort to buy votes around what is otherwise damaging legislation.

This bill blocks millions of acres from new oil and gas leasing and all other business activity. Further, the bill designates more than 2 million acres as wilderness acres, permanently restricting public access. The Federal Government already owns 30 percent of the total land area of the United States. It doesn't need any more.

Though I will not vote for the Omnibus Public Lands bill for the serious reasons previously stated, there are some supportable measures in the bill. The Tuolumne Me-Wuk Land Transfer Act , the Madera Water Supply Enhancement Act , and the San Joaquin River Restoration Settlement are three examples.

The Madera Water Supply Enhancement Act creates an underground water bank in my district which is desperately needed in the San Joaquin Valley to mitigate the effects of drought and the onerous Endangered Species Act regulations.

I also support the San Joaquin River Restoration Settlement, resolving a 20-year lawsuit that threatened the water supply for farmers in the San Joaquin Valley. The San Joaquin River Restoration Settlement gave my agricultural constituents something they did not previously have: a seat at the negotiating table. Before the settlement, a Federal judge was going to decide how much water farmers would lose in order to restore a salmon fishery. By giving farmers a voice in the solution, the settlement prevents an agricultural disaster and gives the agricultural community some control over their water future. Additionally, all 22 water districts of the Friant Water Users Authority have consistently voted in support of the settlement. The settlement is a product of hardworking folks who simply want to continue growing food to feed this great Nation with a safe, reliable, and efficient water supply. I believe we have accomplished that goal in this settlement.

The SPEAKER pro tempore. The gentleman's time has expired.

Ms. FOXX. I yield another 30 seconds to the gentleman from California.

Mr. RADANOVICH. Madam Speaker, I support these portions of the Omnibus Public Lands Act , and believe that they should be passed on their own merit. However, for reasons stated above, I cannot support the overall package and urge my colleagues to vote against this rule that did not allow a vote to save 80,000 jobs and over $2 million in income in California at no cost to the taxpayers.

The following is a congressional speech introducing "The Energy Independence Now Act of 2009."

Mr. BURTON of Indiana. Madam Speaker, I rise today to introduce a bill titled, "The Energy Independence Now Act of 2009."

Few things affect American consumers like high energy prices. During the summer of 2008 with the price of oil hovering near $150 a barrel, Americans faced record prices at the gas pump—in many cases well over $4.00 per gallon. These high prices contributed to a downturn in economic growth, an increase in inflation and forced many American families to make difficult financial choices. According to the latest figures from the Energy Information Administration, gasoline prices are down to around $2 per gallon and the price of oil is close to $50 per barrel. Though the price of gasoline has decreased significantly, many are still concerned that it will rise again and quite possibly because of the disproportionate amount of oil that we import from regimes that are unfriendly to us.

The old adage goes that those who do not learn from history are doomed to repeat it. Apart from creating the Strategic Petroleum Reserves after the oil embargoes of the 1970s, the United States did painfully little to make sure that oil could never again be used as a weapon against us. If anything, we put ourselves further under the thumb of foreign oil. In 1972, we imported approximately 28 percent of the oil we consume from foreign countries; today the United States imports 62 percent of its oil from other nations. While half of that amount comes from our friends in Mexico and Canada, the other half of our imported oil travels from unstable, undemocratic or unfriendly regimes. That means that every time I fill up my gas tank—whether the price is $2 a gallon or $4 a gallon—at least half of my money goes into the economies of Saudi Arabia, Venezuela, Nigeria, and Angola. And while the tactics of oil manipulation may change—price spikes versus an outright embargo—the results are eerily the same.

That is why I am introducing this bill, to continue to move our country forward on the path toward breaking America's dependence on foreign sources of oil while at the same time investing in a renewable energy future. My colleagues on the other side of the aisle are looking to pass a costly cap-and-trade program that will only serve to increase the price of energy for the American consumer and devastate energy companies in my home State of Indiana. Now is not the time to burden families with higher energy costs, when many of them are already struggling to find and keep jobs, pay for college and provide for their families.

I believe that in the long-run we need to get off oil and that requires more investment in alternative energy and energy conservation technologies. My bill addressed this through provisions that would increase alternative energy sources and diversify the energy grid with currently available alternative energy technologies. As a nation, we waste far too much energy with inefficient engines and machines. That is why my bill would provide tax incentives for companies to produce fuel efficient vehicles. In fact, it provides a $500 tax credit for individuals who purchase hybrid cars made by American-based companies.

However, while we are discovering new, clean and cost-effective ways to increase the American energy supply, we must recognize that oil will remain a part of our energy mix for some time. The good news about this is that we have plenty of it. The Department of the Interior, DOI, conducted a comprehensive inventory of oil and natural gas resources located off our coastlines within the last several years, and according to the Department's figures there is an estimated 8.5 billion barrels of known oil reserves and 29.3 trillion cubic feet, tcf, of known natural gas reserves along our coastlines; with 82 percent of the oil and 95 percent of the gas located in the Gulf of Mexico, GOM. However, even more importantly, the Department of the Interior estimates that there are untapped resources of about 86 billion barrels, 51 percent in the Gulf of Mexico, and 420 trillion cubic feet of natural gas, 55 percent in the Gulf of Mexico, out there. My bill would open up these areas to access these resources. Domestic production of these resources would provide much-needed real energy jobs without any cost to the taxpayer.

In addition, my bill opens up the Arctic National Wildlife Refuge, ANWR , which holds the single largest deposit of oil in the entire United States. Its 10.4 billion barrels of oil is more than double the proven reserves of the entire State of Texas and almost half of the total proven reserves in the U.S., 22 billion barrels. Had President Clinton not vetoed ANWR energy production in 1995, the United States could be getting nearly 1.5 million barrels of oil per day from the arctic right now.

In addition, the U.S. has been called the Saudi Arabia of oil shale. It has been estimated that oil shale deposits in Colorado, Utah, and Wyoming hold the equivalent of as little as 1.8 trillion barrels of oil and potentially as much as 8 trillion barrels of oil. In comparison, Saudi Arabia reportedly holds proved reserves of 267 billion barrels. Unfortunately, oil-shale is rough equivalent to diesel fuel and a number of Clean Air Act regulations—such as low-sulfur diesel—and federal motor fuel taxes—which favor gasoline over diesel fuels—have created a strong financial disincentive regarding the production and use of oil-shale fuels. Many of these deposits are on public land making it more bureaucratically complicated to exploit this resource. My bill would provide a financial incentive for companies to invest in and produce more oil from oil shale.

Getting more domestic oil on the market is only half the solution. We haven't built a new refinery in this country in more than 25 years because the approval process for new refinery construction is estimated to require up to 800 different permits. While existing refineries have undergone significant expansion over the years, even as others have been shuttered, our aging refinery infrastructure leaves little margin for error. If we begin to produce more domestic crude oil we would need to turn it into home heating oil, gasoline, or diesel through the refining process. The ability to refine oil must keep pace with the demand for gasoline and diesel. My bill would create an expedited process for the construction of new refining capacity by streamlining the permitting process and opening up closed military bases for construction.

Clearly, developing new oil fields and refineries will take some time. In the interim my bill also helped promote the production of non-food sources for biofuels. It also opens up Federal land for the production of biofuel crops in order to provide relief from high food prices that have resulted from ethanol production.

Madam Speaker, I believe in conservation, I believe in energy efficiency, and I believe in diversifying our energy supply by using wind, solar, coal-to-liquid technologies, ethanol and other renewable energy sources. But the fact of the matter is that oil and natural gas are still going to be a part of our energy mix for a long time to come and we must be able to access our own resources rather than becoming more dependent on unstable parts of the world.

I would like to urge my colleagues to join me in co-sponsoring this important legislation to help America get on the road towards energy independence and to create real jobs at no cost to the taxpayer.

Source D

Muir, John. *Our National Parks*. Houghton, Mifflin, and Company: New York, 1901.

The following is John Muir, a noted environmentalist and founder of the Sierra Club.

The tendency nowadays to wander in wildernesses is delightful to see. Thousands of tired, nerve-shaken, over-civilized people are beginning to find out that going to the mountains is going home; that wildness is a necessity; and that mountain parks and reservations are useful not only as fountains of timber and irrigating rivers, but as fountains of life. Awakening from the stupefying effects of the vice of over-industry and the deadly apathy of luxury, they are trying as best they can to mix and enrich their own little ongoings with those of Nature, and to get rid of rust and disease. Briskly venturing and roaming, some are washing off sins and cobweb cares of the devil's spinning in all-day storms on mountains; sauntering in rosiny pinewoods or in gentian meadows, brushing through chaparral, bending down and parting sweet, flowery sprays; tracing rivers to their sources, getting in touch with the nerves of Mother Earth; jumping from rock to rock, feeling the life of them, learning the songs of them, panting in whole-souled exercise, and rejoicing in deep, long-drawn breaths of pure wildness. This is fine and natural and full of promise. So also is the growing interest in the care and preservation of forests and wild places in general, and in the half wild parks and gardens of towns. Even the scenery habit in its most artificial forms, mixed with spectacles, silliness, and kodaks; its devotees arrayed more gorgeously than scarlet tanagers, frightening the wild game with red umbrellas,—even this is encouraging, and may well be regarded as a hopeful sign of the times.

Source E

Cong. Rec. 3 Feb. 2009: S1430. PDF.

The following is a letter presented for inclusion in the Congressional Record by Senator Crapo of Idaho.

I want to encourage you to not support drilling in ANWR or any currently protected Alaska lands. The high gas prices and our dependence on foreign oil have been hard to stomach, but I believe there are necessary lessons learned for the public. We must decrease our insatiable thirst for natural resources in this country. High gas and fuel prices have made people think hard about changing their driving habits and some of their domestic habits as well. Idaho Power has been encouraging conservation for a few years now, much to their merit, but I do not know how successful their campaign has been. There have not been any great heating/cooling crises yet such as brown or black outs to push people to change.

Personally, I carpool to work with my husband just about every day, unless I am on call (I work in a hospital). Even though I work eight hour days and my husband works nine hour days, I either walk over to his office and wait for him to finish, I bring my running gear and take a run while waiting for him, or I find something else to keep me busy for that extra hour. Sure it's a little inconvenient. I have animals to feed, pastures, a yard, and a garden to water and tend to, and the usual chores one has waiting for them at the end of a work day. However, I believe this small sacrifice is one I can shoulder. Additionally, this means that I only have to fill my small truck once a month. On other days, I try to ride my bike to the store, post office, etc., rather than making an extra car trip. If I have errands to run in my car, I will combine trips into one big loop, on one day, to minimize the amount and time I need to be driving. As far as our consumption of energy at home, we are fortunate enough to have lots of shade trees, a well insulated house, blinds on all of our windows, and an efficient attic fan to keep our house relatively cool on hot days. Last summer during the extensive heat wave we experienced here in SW Idaho I charted the high temperature for the day and the time our AC came on for about 6 weeks. We keep our thermostat set at 79 degrees while we are at work and decrease it to 76 or 77 for the 6 pm to 10 pm time period. We were able to keep our house cool enough 99 percent of those over 100 degree days that the AC didn't come on until after 6 pm and ran only one to two cycles before we were able to open up our windows to cool to outside temps, which by 10 pm were usually below 77 degrees. Our energy bill remained low for the whole summer due to our conservation methods. I am doing the same this summer.

I would like to add that, although I oppose drilling in our last wilderness areas, I fully support conservation incentives and ramping up research and support for alternative energy sources, including nuclear. I hope the proposed nuclear plant in Elmore County receives enough positive support from the public to go ahead. Nuclear energy technologies have advanced a lot since the 70's. I believe with some education for the general public about its increased safety nuclear energy can greatly reduce our dependency on hydrocarbon sources of energy.

ANGELA CALLAHAN, *Eagle.*

The following is a bulletin released by the State of Wisconsin.

THE LAND USE DEBATE

The debate over the state's role in land use planning defies the stereotypical "liberal" or "conservative" alignments. Environmentalists, for example, may favor state or federal control of land use planning and development because they are suspicious of capricious action by local government and its parochial view of planning. On the other hand, they may prefer local control in the case of certain emotionally charged issues, such as the disposal of toxic waste, because they find it easier to mobilize local residents than to persuade a state or regional land use body to reopen debate on a difficult decision already taken.

Business, too, can see advantages on both sides of the debate about local vs. state control of land use. Business owners may prefer to conduct their affairs unhampered by a state land use agency, but they recognize state involvement in land use planning can work to their advantage by overriding local objections to development, creating predictability for landowners or providing statewide tax incentives, such as those for farmland preservation and reclamation.

Proponents. Those favoring a greater state role in land use planning tend to see the issue as crucial to the quality of life of the state. They cite numerous evils that can arise from strictly local control of land use decisions. For example, they claim urban sprawl results from development by private interests who design commercial, residential and recreational projects without consideration of their broader impacts. Unplanned development, they contend, creates problems that ultimately become state concerns. Failure to plan for infrastructure requirements, such as roads, water and sewers, can cost state and local governments valuable tax dollars. Poorly planned development patterns have also caused racial and economic segregation in their view.

Proponents of statewide or regional planning claim that forcing developers and local communities to consider the broader implications of their actions can promote communitywide benefits over parochial concerns. A state plan, or even local decisions made within the framework of state controls, may inhibit the creation of disjointed, unattractive communities that increase pollution, destroy resources and raise infrastructure costs. Supporters of state land use planning point to the simple fact that some problems relating to land use are regional and, therefore, require neighboring local governments to work together.

Opponents. Those opposing a greater state role in land use planning base their opposition on a number of factors. Chief among these is the issue of local control. The creation of a state role in land use decisions necessarily dilutes the power of local governments. Some are suspicious of any transfer of power to a higher level of government. They claim the individuals making land use decisions at the grassroots level have a better opportunity to familiarize themselves with the details of land use situations that may arise; local governments often have a better idea of the needs of the community than do regional or state governments. Opponents of state land use planning also raise the specter of a land use bureaucracy, appointed not elected, wielding great power over the permissible use and, therefore, the value of land. Critics of state-level planning fear that state government will not give sufficient consideration to local interests when making land use decisions. They worry that decisions may have a highly negative impact on local economies and the potential revenue that property development can provide for local governments. Opponents of state land use schemes argue state plans that restrict land to agricultural use can be a threat to farmers who depend on the development value of their land for retirement and to secure credit. Environmental restrictions that might be imposed by a state land use agency also can make farming more difficult.

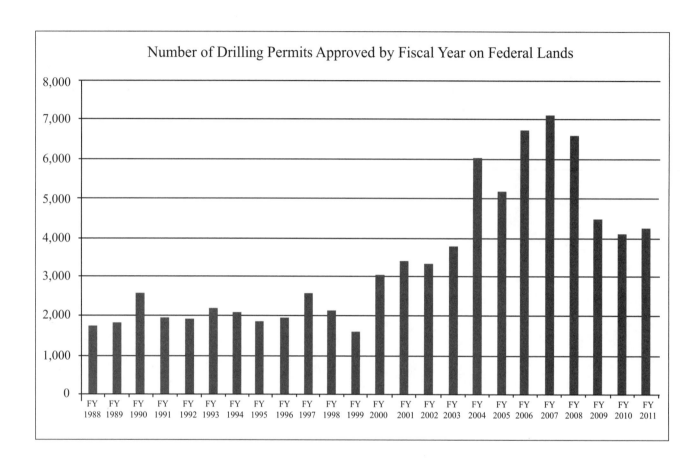

Number of Drilling Permits Approved by Fiscal Year on Federal Lands

English Language and Composition
Synthesis Prompt

Sample Question 3
(Suggested time: 40 minutes. This question will count
for one-third of your total essay section score.)

The role of the newspaper in American society has been multifaceted: among other things, it has disseminated news, served as a forum for opinion, and been a vehicle for commerce. Recently, however, the Internet and online websites have changed the traditional role of the newspaper, with more people using digital resources to receive their news.

Read the following seven sources carefully. Then, synthesize the information from at least three of the sources and compose a well-written essay in which you take a position on the relevancy of the print newspaper in today's society.

Make sure your argument is central to the essay. Be sure to use the sources provided to help elucidate and support your position. While it is not necessary that you use the MLA or APA format in citing your sources, you should clearly identify those sources that you use to help develop and support your opinion. You may identify these sources by referring to the as Source A, B, C, etc., or you may provide identifying information in parenthesis.

Source A (Maloney)
Source B (Smith)
Source C (Lance)
Source D (McMillen)
Source E (United States)
Source F (Advertisement)
Source G (Hathorn)

Source A
Cong. Rec. 17 Sept. 2009: E2313. PDF.

The following is commentary from Congresswoman Maloney on the "Newspaper Revitalization Act of 2009."

Mrs. MALONEY. Madam Speaker, today I am introducing the "Newspaper Revitalization Act of 2009," the companion to legislation introduced in the Senate by Senator CARDIN (D-MD). This legislation will help newspapers across the country that are closing down or facing bankruptcy at an alarming rate by allowing them to become non-profit 501(c)(3) organizations similar to public broadcasting. Large cities whose newspapers include, The Philadelphia Inquirer, The Seattle Post-Intelligencer, The Rocky Mountain News, San Francisco Chronicle, and The Baltimore Sun are at risk of losing their dailies. Unless something is done soon, it is possible that many metropolitan regions may have no local daily newspapers .

Many bloggers, Google news, and punditry get their original news from the diligent work of beat reporters for daily newspapers who have invested years on their beat and provide the best information on an issue from many perspectives. This type of beat reporting requires commitments of both time and money, and unfortunately, the current economic climate has only worsened the already precarious business situation for many newspapers . This bill would provide for a voluntary option for newspapers and a way for a community or foundations to step in and preserve their local papers that are rapidly disappearing.

Newspapers are an essential component to our free democratic society. Studies have shown that areas where daily newspapers have gone out of business there has been a rise in corruption in government and plummeting civil engagement in politics. With the state of the current newspaper model, dependent on advertising and circulation revenue, it will be difficult for newspapers to maintain and produce high quality news without bold changes. I urge my colleagues to support this legislation as an important first step in saving them.

Source B

<u>Cong. Rec.</u> 23 June 2009: E1537. PDF.

The following is commentary from Congressman Smith regarding bias in newspaper stories.

Mr. SMITH of Texas. Madam Speaker, in some national newspapers , the line between news reporting and opinion has become non-existent. Take two recent examples:

First, this opinionated sentence from The Washington Post on America's health care system: ``Nowhere else in the world is so much money spent with such poor results."

Second, this sarcastic comment from The New York Times on Supreme Court nominee Judge Sotomayor: ``Of course, it is not as if a lawyer and judge with a history of involvement in racial issues has not made it onto the Supreme Court. Thurgood Marshall, a fierce advocate for racial justice as a lawyer for the NAACP, sailed onto the highest bench in the 1960s."

Amazingly, these blatant opinions are from front-page news stories, not editorials.

Newspapers should report the facts and save opinions for the editorial page.

Source C

Cong. Rec. 12 Jan. 2010: E9. PDF.

The following is from Congressman Lance commenting on an online news source.

Mr. LANCE. Madam Speaker, I rise today to congratulate The AlternativePress.com as it celebrates its one-year anniversary.

The AlternativePress.com was launched in October 2008 and currently serves as New Jersey's all-online alternative to local print newspapers.

In my congressional district, The AlternativePress.com serves residents in Berkeley Heights, New Providence, Summit and Westfield and features a wide array of news and information, from video streaming of local high school sports events to real estate listings and restaurant reviews, to objective local, regional and state news.

The AlternativePress.com is led by lifelong New Jersey resident and Rutgers University graduate Michael M. Shapiro, who serves as the outlet's chief executive officer and editor.

I would like to congratulate Michael Shapiro and the entire AlternativePress.com team as it celebrates its one-year anniversary. I commend the whole team for its tremendous service to the public.

The following is from a government blog sponsored by the National Archives.

Today, the challenges to journalism are technological, financial, and personal; and the stake for society is monumental.

Investigative journalism is the crown jewel of journalism. Awards from the Pulitzer Prize to the Ridenhour Prizes Fostering the Spirit of Courage and Truth reward individuals and institutions that excel in providing the public insights they would be hard pressed to gain on their own. Investigative journalism, however, is expensive.

As the economics of news have changed, those institutions that once subsidized these efforts have come under increasing pressure. Some have gone bankrupt. Others have merged or contracted their services. Somewhere between 17,000 and 18,000 jobs in journalism disappeared between 2008 and 2010. [My source, of course, is a Blog, not a newspaper article: Paper Cuts.]

How do we ensure that journalists in their zeal to write about government are better informed about critical issues of accessing today's government records?

Technology provides part of the answer. Today, computing power allows the mashup of information in ways that was once available only to the Homeland Security Department or the CIA. Jay Hamilton, director of the DeWitt Wallace Center for Media and Democracy at Duke University, recently pointed out that journalists identified convicted drug dealers employed as school bus drivers and public officials giving themselves property tax discounts by combining and combing through disparate government data sets.

IT research is developing advanced tools that allow investigative reporters to access and analyze records for accurate reporting.

These and other issues facing public access to government information will be explored in depth at the Media Access to Government Information Conference on April 12, 2011 at the National Archives in downtown Washington, DC.

The goal of the conference is to discuss how technology might improve access to government information for journalists and citizens alike.

The following is commentary from a governmental website.

The information age is fueling the expansion and development of reliable information and communications technology (ICT) systems and services throughout the world. Ambitious plans are under way in many countries, and U.S. firms are poised to supply needed technology and equipment. USTDA furthers the development of this sector by funding various forms of technical assistance, early investment analysis, training, reverse trade missions and business workshops that support the development of a modern infrastructure and a fair and open trading environment.

In fiscal year 2008, USTDA invested in 17 new activities in the ICT sector.

The following is an advertisement that appeared in Hearst Newspapers in the 1920s.

The following is an image from Wikipedia Commons.

The Analysis Essay

Introduction

Many of the skills needed to be successful on the AP® English Language and Composition Examination analysis essay have already been targeted in the multiple-choice section of this manual. Specifically, you should be able to ascertain information regarding the speaker, the intended audience, the purpose of the passage and its overarching argument by using those strategies discussed previously. Additionally, the information regarding a passage's structure, tone, rhetorical strategies, and diction and syntax choice are also intricately tied to your success in analyzing and responding to the analysis prompt on the exam. It is important that you review this section of the manual in concert with the following strategies so that you will be successful.

To respond to the analysis essay, you will be asked to read and analyze a lengthy passage from a work of nonfiction. You may be presented with a passage from an autobiography, a biography, a letter, a speech, or a historical document of significance. You may even be provided two shorter passages from these genres and asked to compare and contrast the different attitudes each respective speaker has to his or her subject matter.

Regardless of the passage or passages, you will need to manage your time appropriately so that you can read, plan and compose your response within a 40-minute time frame. Even with the 15-minute reading period, it is essential that you be as judicious with your time as possible.

Approaching the Analysis Prompt

Annotating the Text

As discussed earlier, it is absolutely critical that you annotate the text as you are reading it. Making note of rhetorical devices, shifts in tone, and other critical elements of the passage is an essential part of actively reading a text and will greatly aid the planning and composition steps of your response, saving you valuable time. You are not expected to be able—particularly given the time constraints—to identify every single rhetorical strategy or syntactical element found within the text. You should, however, hone in on each paragraph and identify at least one, if not several, rhetorical devices utilized in the work. You should also consider patterns and be able to recognize and identify those strategies that the speaker utilizes most frequently within the passage.

Ultimately, how you choose to annotate the text is entirely up to you. However, specific strategies are provided in the multiple-choice section of this guide. Please note, those students who are most successful, not only on the exam as a whole but also on the analysis prompt, annotate the text carefully and frequently. They engage with the text as an active reader, and their comments and notations often help to shed light and meaning on the passage as a whole. You are encouraged to follow in their footsteps.

The T-Chart

The T-Chart is a frequently used organizational tool that you, no doubt, have been introduced to before. For our purposes, the T-chart offers a simple but meaningful organizational tool with which to plan your response to the analysis prompt on the AP® exam. The T-chart is best used, as are all of the following strategies, in conjunction with a well-annotated passage. To use the T-chart, create a four-quadrant chart. Label the upper left quadrant "argument" and the upper right quadrant "rhetorical strategies." After reading and annotating a sample passage, articulate either the purpose or the argument in the lower left hand quadrant, and list, in chronological order, the rhetorical strategies and devices most prevalent in the passage. In doing so, you have thereby eliminated superfluous annotations and have created a rough outline for your response to the analysis prompt.

Please note, those essays that are more successful are not organized according to rhetorical devices. In other words, less successful essays tend to use the rhetorical strategies as organizational devices. There may be an entire paragraph devoted to metaphor, another to repetition, and so on. The successful essay focuses on the organization of the argument itself, rather than on a categorized list of strategies employed by the speaker. Therefore, the T-chart is useful in providing you with a prewriting tool that focuses on the ways in which rhetorical strategies are employed by a speaker to further his or her argument as it develops, rather than the strategies themselves.

Consider the following passage. Annotate it and complete a T-chart.

Concession to opposing viewpoints

MR. PRESIDENT: No man thinks more highly than I do of the patriotism, as well as abilities, of the very worthy gentlemen who have just addressed the House. But different men often see the same subject in different lights; and, therefore, I hope it will not be thought disrespectful to those gentlemen if, entertaining as I do, opinions of a character very opposite to theirs, I shall speak forth my sentiments freely, and without reserve. This is no time for ceremony. The question before the House is one of awful moment to this country. For my own part, I consider it as nothing less than a question of freedom or slavery; and in proportion to the magnitude of the subject ought to be the freedom of the debate. It is only in this way that we can hope to arrive at truth, and fulfil the great responsibility which we hold to God and our country. Should I keep back my opinions at such a time, through fear of giving offence, I should consider myself as guilty of treason towards my country, and of an act of disloyalty toward the majesty of heaven, which I revere above all earthly kings.

allusion

rhetorical questioning

Mr. President, it is natural to man to indulge in the illusions of hope. We are apt to shut our eyes against a painful truth, and listen to the song of that siren till she transforms us into beasts. Is this the part of wise men, engaged in a great and arduous struggle for liberty? Are we disposed to be of the number of those who, having eyes, see not, and, having ears, hear not, the things which so nearly concern their temporal salvation? For my part, whatever anguish of spirit it may cost, I am willing to know the whole truth; to know the worst, and to provide for it.

I have but one lamp by which my feet are guided; and that is the lamp of experience. I know of no way of judging of the future but by the past. And judging by the past, I wish to know what there has been in the conduct of the British ministry for the last ten years, to justify those hopes with which gentlemen have been pleased to solace themselves, and the House? Is it that insidious smile with which our petition has been lately received? Trust it not, sir; it will prove a snare to your feet. Suffer not yourselves to be betrayed with a kiss. Ask yourselves how this gracious reception of our petition comports with these war-like preparations which cover our waters and darken our land. Are fleets and armies necessary to a work of love and reconciliation? Have we shown ourselves so unwilling to be reconciled, that force must be called in to win back our love? Let us not deceive ourselves, sir. These are the implements of war and subjugation; the last arguments to which kings resort. I ask, gentlemen, sir, what means this martial array, if its purpose be not to force us to submission? Can gentlemen assign any other possible motive for it? Has Great Britain any enemy, in this quarter of the world, to call for all this accumulation of navies and armies? No, sir, she has none. They are meant for us; they can be meant for no other. They are sent over to bind and rivet upon us those chains which the British ministry have been so long forging. And what have we to oppose to them? Shall we try argument? Sir, we have been trying that for the last ten years. Have we anything new to offer upon the subject? Nothing. We have held the subject up in every light of which it is capable; but it has been all in vain. Shall we resort to entreaty and humble supplication? What terms shall we find which have not been already exhausted? Let us not, I beseech you, sir, deceive ourselves. Sir, we have done everything that could be done, to avert the storm which is now coming on. We have petitioned; we have remonstrated; we have supplicated; we have prostrated ourselves before the throne, and have implored its interposition to arrest the tyrannical hands of the ministry and Parliament. Our petitions have been slighted; our remonstrances have produced additional violence and insult; our supplications have been disregarded; and we have been spurned, with contempt, from the foot of the throne. In vain, after these things, may we indulge the fond hope of peace and reconciliation. There is no longer any room for hope. If we wish to be free if we mean to preserve inviolate those inestimable privileges for which we have been so long contending if we mean not basely to abandon the noble struggle in which we have been so long engaged, and which we have pledged ourselves never to abandon until the glorious object of our contest shall be obtained, we must fight! I repeat it, sir, we must fight! An appeal to arms and to the God of Hosts is all that is left us!

They tell us, sir, that we are weak; unable to cope with so formidable an adversary. But when shall we be stronger? Will it be the next week, or the next year? Will it be when we are totally disarmed, and when a British guard shall be stationed in every house? Shall we gather strength by irresolution

historical precedent

more rhetorical questioning

continual use of us/we connects speaker to audience

still more rhetorical questioning

imagery-slavery

listing to emphasize previous strategies employed to avert conflict

looming specter of quartering

and inaction? Shall we acquire the means of effectual resistance, by lying supinely on our backs, and hugging the delusive phantom of hope, until our enemies shall have bound us hand and foot? Sir, we are not weak if we make a proper use of those means which the God of nature hath placed in our power. Three millions of people, armed in the holy cause of liberty, and in such a country as that which we possess, are invincible by any force which our enemy can send against us. Besides, sir, we shall not fight our battles alone. There is a just God who presides over the destinies of nations; and who will raise up friends to fight our battles for us. The battle, sir, is not to the strong alone; it is to the vigilant, the active, the brave. Besides, sir, we have no election. If we were base enough to desire it, it is now too late to retire from the contest. There is no retreat but in submission and slavery! Our chains are forged! Their clanking may be heard on the plains of Boston! The war is inevitable and let it come! I repeat it, sir, let it come.

It is in vain, sir, to extenuate the matter. Gentlemen may cry, Peace, Peace but there is no peace. The war is actually begun! The next gale that sweeps from the north will bring to our ears the clash of resounding arms! Our brethren are already in the field! Why stand we here idle? What is it that gentlemen wish? What would they have? Is life so dear, or peace so sweet, as to be purchased at the price of chains and slavery? Forbid it, Almighty God! I know not what course others may take; but as for me, give me liberty or give me death!

—from Speech at the Virginia Convention by Patrick Henry

Argument or Purpose	Rhetorical Strategies
"War is already at hand and slavery is not an acceptable price for peace. The time for action is now."	Concession Allusion Rhetorical questions First person pronoun use Slavery imagery Listing References to God Call to Arms

As you can see, the T-chart provides a quick method for organizing and examining a passage's key rhetorical features. The left-hand column asks you to hone in on the overall argument or purpose of the passage, while the right-hand column zeros in on those strategies used most frequently to develop the argument.

Rhetorical Parts

An organizational strategy that can be used in conjunction with a T-chart is the breaking up of a passage into its rhetorical "parts." A simple way of considering the rhetorical parts of a passage is to consider and label the role that each paragraph plays in the development of a passage's argument. While a paragraph analysis provides an easy way to divide a passage into parts, it is not, however, the most nuanced strategy.

A nuanced approach to breaking a passage into its component rhetorical parts considers not only visual breaks as provided by paragraphs, but also the shifts in the development of the argument itself. Consider the various ways in which Patrick Henry's speech to the Virginia convention shifts as the speaker develops his argument.

Speaker here is establishing his trustworthiness

{MR. PRESIDENT: No man thinks more highly than I do of the patriotism, as well as abilities, of the very worthy gentlemen who have just addressed the House. But different men often see the same subject in different lights; and, therefore, I hope it will not be thought disrespectful to those gentlemen if, entertaining as I do, opinions of a character very opposite to theirs, I shall speak forth my sentiments freely, and without reserve. This is no time for ceremony. The question before the House is one of awful moment to this country. For my own part, I consider it as nothing less than a question of freedom or slavery; and in proportion to the magnitude of the subject ought to be the freedom of the debate. It is only in this way that we can hope to arrive at truth, and fulfil the great responsibility which we hold to God and our country. Should I keep back my opinions at such a time, through fear of giving offence, I should consider myself as guilty of treason towards my country, and of an act of disloyalty toward the majesty of heaven, which I revere above all earthly kings.}

Logic—reasons peace is not an option

{Mr. President, it is natural to man to indulge in the illusions of hope. We are apt to shut our eyes against a painful truth, and listen to the song of that siren till she transforms us into beasts. Is this the part of wise men, engaged in a great and arduous struggle for liberty? Are we disposed to be of the number of those who, having eyes, see not, and, having ears, hear not, the things which so nearly concern their temporal salvation? For my part, whatever anguish of spirit it may cost, I am willing to know the whole truth; to know the worst, and to provide for it.

I have but one lamp by which my feet are guided; and that is the lamp of experience. I know of no way of judging of the future but by the past. And judging by the past, I wish to know what there has been in the conduct of the British ministry for the last ten years, to justify those hopes with which gentlemen have been pleased to solace themselves, and the House? Is it that insidious smile with which our petition has been lately received? Trust it not, sir; it will prove a snare to your feet. Suffer not yourselves to be betrayed with a kiss. Ask yourselves how this gracious reception of our petition comports with these war-like preparations which cover our waters and darken our land. Are fleets and armies necessary to a work of love and reconciliation? Have we shown ourselves so unwilling to be reconciled, that force must be called in to win back our love? Let us not deceive ourselves, sir. These are the implements of war and subjugation; the last arguments to which kings resort. I ask, gentlemen, sir, what means this martial array, if its purpose be not to force us to submission? Can gentlemen assign any other possible motive for it? Has

Great Britain any enemy, in this quarter of the world, to call for all this accumulation of navies and armies? No, sir, she has none. They are meant for us; they can be meant for no other. They are sent over to bind and rivet upon us those chains which the British ministry have been so long forging. And what have we to oppose to them? Shall we try argument? Sir, we have been trying that for the last ten years. Have we anything new to offer upon the subject? Nothing. We have held the subject up in every light of which it is capable; but it has been all in vain. Shall we resort to entreaty and humble supplication? What terms shall we find which have not been already exhausted? Let us not, I beseech you, sir, deceive ourselves. Sir, we have done everything that could be done, to avert the storm which is now coming on. We have petitioned; we have remonstrated; we have supplicated; we have prostrated ourselves before the throne, and have implored its interposition to arrest the tyrannical hands of the ministry and Parliament. Our petitions have been slighted; our remonstrances have produced additional violence and insult; our supplications have been disregarded; and we have been spurned, with contempt, from the foot of the throne. In vain, after these things, may we indulge the fond hope of peace and reconciliation. There is no longer any room for hope. } { If we wish to be free if we mean to preserve inviolate those inestimable privileges for which we have been so long contending if we mean not basely to abandon the noble struggle in which we have been so long engaged, and which we have pledged ourselves never to abandon until the glorious object of our contest shall be obtained, we must fight! I repeat it, sir, we must fight! An appeal to arms and to the God of Hosts is all that is left us!

They tell us, sir, that we are weak; unable to cope with so formidable an adversary. But when shall we be stronger? Will it be the next week, or the next year? Will it be when we are totally disarmed, and when a British guard shall be stationed in every house? Shall we gather strength by irresolution and inaction? Shall we acquire the means of effectual resistance, by lying supinely on our backs, and hugging the delusive phantom of hope, until our enemies shall have bound us hand and foot? Sir, we are not weak if we make a proper use of those means which the God of nature hath placed in our power. Three millions of people, armed in the holy cause of liberty, and in such a country as that which we possess, are invincible by any force which our enemy can send against us. Besides, sir, we shall not fight our battles alone. There is a just God who presides over the destinies of nations; and who will raise up friends to fight our battles for us. The battle, sir, is not to the strong alone; it is to the vigilant, the active, the brave. Besides, sir, we have no election. If we were base enough to desire it, it is now too late to retire from the contest. There is no retreat but in submission and slavery! Our chains are forged! Their clanking may be heard on the plains of Boston! The war is inevitable and let it come! I repeat it, sir, let it come.

It is in vain, sir, to extenuate the matter. Gentlemen may cry, Peace, Peace but there is no peace. The war is actually begun! The next gale that sweeps from the north will bring to our ears the clash of resounding arms! Our brethren are already in the field! Why stand we here idle? What is it that

Call to arms

gentlemen wish? What would they have? Is life so dear, or peace so sweet, as to be purchased at the price of chains and slavery? Forbid it, Almighty God! I know not what course others may take; but as for me, give me liberty or give me death! }

When you consider the rhetorical parts of a passage, you are, in essence, providing an organizational framework for your own essay in response to the prompt. In the case of the Henry speech, given the examples above, one might devise a five paragraph essay organized around the three "parts" of the speech: the introduction that establishes the speaker's credentials, the factual analysis that examines the crisis faced by the colonists, and the call to arms, the speaker's invitation to action. Having used the passage itself to help sculpt the organization of your response, your task is then to discuss those rhetorical strategies used in each of the three parts in the development of the speaker's argument itself. This is a far better approach to responding to the analysis question than dedicating paragraphs to the specific strategies.

The Aristotelian Triangle

Aristotle's art of rhetoric can prove helpful when applied to rhetorical analysis. Aristotelian logic asks the reader to examine three key components of a work: the trustworthiness of its speaker, referred to as ethos; the logic of its argument, referred to as logos; and the emotional impact it has on its audience, referred to as pathos. Reflecting on these three components can be useful when analyzing a passage.

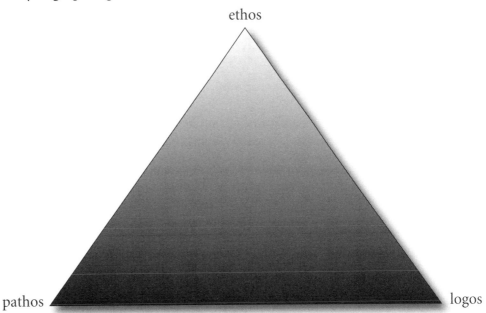

Therefore, one organizational strategy you might consider is the above graphic organizer, the Aristotelian triangle. Under each point, you should list examples from the passage that appeal to the emotions, logic, or trustworthiness respectively. For example, consider the completed Aristotelian triangle for Patrick Henry's speech to the Virginia convention.

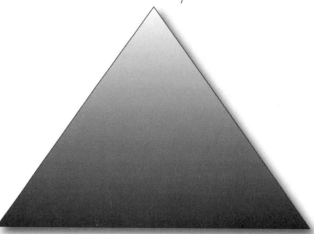

Ethos: issues a concession, makes use of first person plural to connect with audience, alludes to a shared belief system

Pathos: rhetorical questioning, imagery, repetition and parallel construction, anaphora

Logos: discusses existing tyranny, British ships in American harbors, British armament, and the fact that all previous requests for representation have been slighted by the British

The Rhetorical Device Box

Another graphic organizer is the rhetorical device box. Rather than focus specifically on the terms ethos, pathos, and logos, this strategy examines each term in a different way by focusing on four components labeled on each of the four sides of a square box: the speaker, the audience, the purpose of the passage, and its argument. Additionally, the rhetorical strategies used by the author can be listed inside the box.

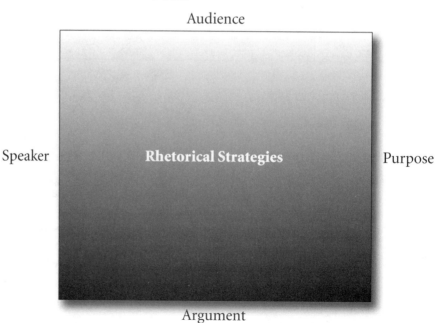

Audience

Speaker

Rhetorical Strategies

Purpose

Argument

Given the time constraints, this can be a particularly useful graphic organizer as each of its component parts explores a significant aspect of the passage. Consider the following questions in articulating each of these components.

Now consider how Patrick Henry's speech once more. This is how you might complete the rhetorical device box for the speech:

1. Speaker—Patrick Henry, Patriot, Values liberty, Impassioned, Respectful.
2. Audience—delegates to the Virginia convention, fellow patriots, those concerned by British policies, those who value freedom and liberty, those who value peace
3. Purpose—To persuade the audience to take up arms against the British
4. Argument—War is already at hand and slavery is not an acceptable price for peace. The time for action is now.
5. Rhetorical Strategies: rhetorical questions, call to arms, concessions, imagery, repetition, anaphora, parallel structure, religious allusions, metaphorical language

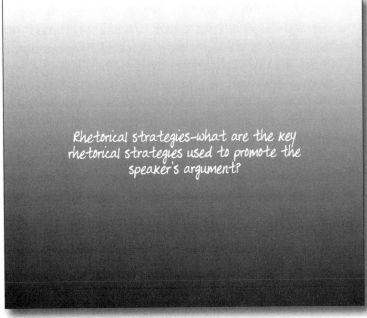

Audience-who is the intended audience? What specific appeals does the speaker make to this audience?

Speaker-what do we know about the speaker? Is the speaker trustworthy? What is the speaker's position on the topic? How do you visualize the speaker? What is the speaker's tone or attitude toward the subject matter?

Rhetorical strategies-what are the key rhetorical strategies used to promote the speaker's argument?

Purpose-what is the reason the speaker has written about this subject matter? What goal does the speaker have?

Argument-what ultimately does this piece argue? What are its claims? What is its thesis?

Sample Analysis Prompts

Sample Question 1

(Suggested time: 40 minutes. This question counts for one-third of the total essay section score.)

The passage below is an excerpt from Malcolm Gladwell's essay "Small Change, Why the Revolution Will Not Be Tweeted." In the essay, Gladwell contends, despite claims to the contrary, social media does not successfully incite social activism to the same degree as those tactics and networks used my men like Martin Luther King during the civil rights movement. Read the passage carefully. Then write an essay in which you analyze the strategies Gladwell uses to develop his position on social media's role in orchestrating social change.

Boycotts and sit-ins and nonviolent confrontations—which were the weapons of choice for the civil-rights movement—are high-risk strategies. They leave little room for conflict and error. The moment even one protester deviates from the script and responds to provocation, the moral legitimacy of the entire

5 protest is compromised. Enthusiasts for social media would no doubt have us believe that King's task in Birmingham would have been made infinitely easier had he been able to communicate with his followers through Facebook, and contented himself with tweets from a Birmingham jail. But networks are messy: think of the ceaseless pattern of correction and revision, amendment

10 and debate, that characterizes Wikipedia. If Martin Luther King, Jr., had tried to do a wikiboycott in Montgomery, he would have been steamrollered by the white power structure. And of what use would a digital communication tool be in a town where ninety-eight per cent of the black community could be reached every Sunday morning at church? The things that King needed in

15 Birmingham—discipline and strategy—were things that online social media cannot provide.

The bible of the social-media movement is Clay Shirky's "Here Comes Everybody." Shirky, who teaches at New York University, sets out to demonstrate the organizing power of the Internet, and he begins with the story of

20 Evan, who worked on Wall Street, and his friend Ivanna, after she left her smart phone, an expensive Sidekick, on the back seat of a New York City taxicab. The telephone company transferred the data on Ivanna's lost phone to a new phone, whereupon she and Evan discovered that the Sidekick was now in the hands of a teen-ager from Queens, who was using it to take photographs of

25 herself and her friends.

When Evan e-mailed the teen-ager, Sasha, asking for the phone back, she replied that his "white ass" didn't deserve to have it back. Miffed, he set up a Web page with her picture and a description of what had happened. He forwarded the link to his friends, and they forwarded it to their friends. Someone

30 found the MySpace page of Sasha's boyfriend, and a link to it found its way onto the site. Someone found her address online and took a video of her home while driving by; Evan posted the video on the site. The story was picked up by

the news filter Digg. Evan was now up to ten e-mails a minute. He created a bulletin board for his readers to share their stories, but it crashed under the weight of responses. Evan and Ivanna went to the police, but the police filed the report under "lost," rather than "stolen," which essentially closed the case. "By this point millions of readers were watching," Shirky writes, "and dozens of mainstream news outlets had covered the story." Bowing to the pressure, the N.Y.P.D. reclassified the item as "stolen." Sasha was arrested, and Evan got his friend's Sidekick back.

Shirky's argument is that this is the kind of thing that could never have happened in the pre-Internet age—and he's right. Evan could never have tracked down Sasha. The story of the Sidekick would never have been publicized. An army of people could never have been assembled to wage this fight. The police wouldn't have bowed to the pressure of a lone person who had misplaced something as trivial as a cell phone. The story, to Shirky, illustrates "the ease and speed with which a group can be mobilized for the right kind of cause" in the Internet age.

Shirky considers this model of activism an upgrade. But it is simply a form of organizing which favors the weak-tie connections that give us access to information over the strong-tie connections that help us persevere in the face of danger. It shifts our energies from organizations that promote strategic and disciplined activity and toward those which promote resilience and adaptability. It makes it easier for activists to express themselves, and harder for that expression to have any impact. The instruments of social media are well suited to making the existing social order more efficient. They are not a natural enemy of the status quo. If you are of the opinion that all the world needs is a little buffing around the edges, this should not trouble you. But if you think that there are still lunch counters out there that need integrating it ought to give you pause.

Shirky ends the story of the lost Sidekick by asking, portentously, "What happens next?"—no doubt imagining future waves of digital protesters. But he has already answered the question. What happens next is more of the same. A networked, weak-tie world is good at things like helping Wall Streeters get phones back from teen-age girls. *Viva la revolución.*

Sample Question 2

(Suggested time: 40 minutes. This question counts for one-third of the total essay section score.)

In the introduction to his essay, "Nature," Ralph Waldo Emerson proclaims that contemporary society is too rooted in impersonal traditions and the past, often manifested in "biographies, histories, and criticism." He, thus, calls for more introspection using nature as a conduit to deeper knowledge. Read the passage carefully. Then write an essay in which you analyze the rhetorical strategies Emerson uses to convey his message about the value of a direct experience with the natural world.

Our age is retrospective. It builds the sepulchres of the fathers. It writes biographies, histories, and criticism. The foregoing generations beheld God and nature face to face; we, through their eyes. Why should not we also enjoy an original relation to the universe? Why should not we have a poetry and philos-
5 ophy of insight and not of tradition, and a religion by revelation to us, and not the history of theirs? Embosomed for a season in nature, whose floods of life stream around and through us, and invite us by the powers they supply, to action proportioned to nature, why should we grope among the dry bones of the past, or put the living generation into masquerade out of its faded
10 wardrobe? The sun shines to-day also. There is more wool and flax in the fields. There are new lands, new men, new thoughts. Let us demand our own works and laws and worship.

Undoubtedly we have no questions to ask which are unanswerable. We must trust the perfection of the creation so far, as to believe that whatever
15 curiosity the order of things has awakened in our minds, the order of things can satisfy. Every man's condition is a solution in hieroglyphic to those inquiries he would put. He acts it as life, before he apprehends it as truth. In like manner, nature is already, in its forms and tendencies, describing its own design. Let us interrogate the great apparition, that shines so peacefully around
20 us. Let us inquire, to what end is nature?

All science has one aim, namely, to find a theory of nature. We have theories of races and of functions, but scarcely yet a remote approach to an idea of creation. We are now so far from the road to truth, that religious teachers dispute and hate each other, and speculative men are esteemed unsound and friv-
25 olous. But to a sound judgment, the most abstract truth is the most practical. Whenever a true theory appears, it will be its own evidence. Its test is, that it will explain all phenomena. Now many are thought not only unexplained but inexplicable; as language, sleep, madness, dreams, beasts, sex.

Philosophically considered, the universe is composed of Nature and the
30 Soul. Strictly speaking, therefore, all that is separate from us, all which Philosophy distinguishes as the NOT ME, that is, both nature and art, all other men and my own body, must be ranked under this name, NATURE. In enumerating the values of nature and casting up their sum, I shall use the word in both

senses;—in its common and in its philosophical import. In inquiries so general
35 as our present one, the inaccuracy is not material; no confusion of thought will
occur. Nature, in the common sense, refers to essences unchanged by man;
space, the air, the river, the leaf. Art is applied to the mixture of his will with the
same things, as in a house, a canal, a statue, a picture. But his operations taken
together are so insignificant, a little chipping, baking, patching, and washing,
40 that in an impression so grand as that of the world on the human mind, they
do not vary the result.

Sample Question 3

(Suggested time: 40 minutes. This question counts for one-third of the total essay section score.)

John Okada, a Japanese-American born in Seattle, Washington, wrote the novel *No-No Boy* to address the internment of Japanese Americans during World War II and the lingering impacts the interment had on the Japanese American community following the war. The following passage is an excerpt from the novel's preface, in which Okada addresses citizens' reactions to the Japanese immediately following the events of December 7, 1941. Read the excerpt carefully. Then write an essay in which you analyze the rhetorical strategies Okada uses to capture the shift in public sentiment toward Japanese Americans.

December the Seventh of the year 1941 was the day when the Japanese bombs fell on Pearl Harbor.

As of that moment, the Japanese in the United States became, by virtue of their ineradicable brownness and the slant eyes which, upon close inspection,
5   will seldom appear slanty, animals of a different breed. The moment the impact of the words solemnly being transmitted over the several million radios of the nation struck home, everything Japanese and everyone Japanese became despicable.

The college professor, finding it suddenly impossible to meet squarely the
10   gaze of his polite, serious, but now too Japanese-ish star pupil, coughed on his pipe and assured the lad that things were a mess. Conviction lacking, he failed at his attempt to be worldly and assuring. He mumbled something about things turning out one way or the other sooner or later and sighed with relief when the little fellow, who hardly ever smiled and, now, probably never would,
15   stood up and left the room.

In a tavern, a drunk, irrigating the sponge in his belly, let it be known to the world that he never thought much about the sneaky Japs and that this proved he was right. It did not matter that he owed his Japanese landlord three-weeks' rent, nor that that industrious Japanese had often picked him off
20   the sidewalk and deposited him on his bed. Someone set up a round of beer for the boys in the place and, further fortified, he announced with patriotic tremor in his alcoholic tones that he would be first in line at the recruiting office the very next morning. That night the Japanese landlord picked him off the sidewalk and put him to bed.

25   A truck and a keen sense of horse-trading had provided a good living for Herman Fine. He bought from and sold primarily to Japanese hotel-keepers and grocers. No transaction was made without considerable haggling and clever maneuvering, for the Japanese could be and often were a shifty lot whose solemn promises frequently turned out to be groundwork for more extended
30   and complex stratagems to cheat him out of his rightful profit. Herman Fine listened to the radio and cried without tears for the Japanese, who, in an instant of time that was not even a speck on the big calendar, had taken their place

beside the Jew. The Jew was used to suffering. The writing for them was etched in caked and dried blood over countless generations upon countless genera-
35 tions. The Japanese did not know. They were proud, too proud, and they were ambitious, too ambitious. Bombs had fallen and, in less time than it takes a Japanese farmer's wife in California to run from the fields into the house and give birth to a child, the writing was scrawled for them. The Jap-Jew would look in the mirror this Sunday night and see a Jap-Jew.

40 The indignation, the hatred, the patriotism of the American people shifted into full-throated condemnation of the Japanese who blotted their land. The Japanese who were born Americans and remained Japanese because biology does not know the meaning of patriotism no longer worried about whether they were Japanese-Americans or American-Japanese. They were
45 Japanese, just as were their Japanese mothers and Japanese fathers and Japanese brothers and sisters. The radio had said as much.

Sample Question 4

(Suggested time: 40 minutes. This question counts for one-third of the total essay section score.)

Read the following two nineteenth-century portrayals of American Indians. Then write an essay in which you analyze how the distinctive style and language of each passage reveals each author's attitude towards America's first inhabitants.

Passage 1

I have for a long time been of opinion, that the wilderness of our country afforded models equal to those from which the Grecian sculptors transferred to the marble such inimitable grace and beauty; and I am now more confirmed in this opinion, since I have immersed myself in the midst of thousands and
5   tens of thousands of these knights of the forest; whose whole lives are lives of chivalry, and whose daily feats, with their naked limbs, might vie with those of the Grecian youths in the beautiful rivalry of the Olympian games.

No man's imagination, with all the aids of description that can be given to it, can ever picture the beauty and wildness of scenes that may be daily wit-
10   nessed in this romantic country; of hundreds of these graceful youths, without a care to wrinkle, or a fear to disturb the full expression of pleasure and enjoyment that beams upon their faces—their long black hair mingling with their horses' tails, floating in the wind, while they are flying over the carpeted prairie, and dealing death with their spears and arrows, to a band of infuriated
15   buffaloes; or their splendid procession in a war-parade, arrayed in all their gorgeous colours and trappings, moving with most exquisite grace and manly beauty, added to that bold defiance which man carries on his front, who acknowledges no superior on earth, and who is amenable to no laws except the laws of God and honour.

—from George Catlin "Letter from the Yellowstone River" (1844)

Passage 2

At the period when "Nick of the Woods" was written, the genius of Chateaubriand and of Cooper had thrown a poetical illusion over the Indian character; and the red men were presented—almost stereotyped in the popular mind—as the embodiments of grand and tender sentiment—a new style of
5   the beau-ideal—brave, gentle, loving, refined, honourable, romantic personages—nature's nobles, the chivalry of the forest. It may be submitted that such are not the lineaments of the race—that they never were the lineaments of any race existing in an uncivilized state—indeed, could not be—and that such conceptions as *Atala* and *Uncas* are beautiful unrealities and fictions merely, as
10   imaginary and contrary to nature as the shepherd swains of the old pastoral school of rhyme and romance; at all events, that one does not find beings of this class, or any thing in the slightest degree resembling them, among the tribes now known to travellers and legislators. The Indian is doubtless a gentleman; but he is a gentleman who wears a very dirty shirt, and lives a very miser-

15 able life, having nothing to employ him or keep him alive except the pleasures of the chase and of the scalp-hunt—which we dignify with the name of war. The writer differed from his critical friends, and from many philanthropists, in believing the Indian to be capable—perfectly capable, where restraint assists the work of friendly instruction—of civilisation: the Choctaws and Cherokees,
20 and the ancient Mexicans and Peruvians, prove it; but, in his natural barbaric state, he is a barbarian—and it is not possible he could be anything else.

—from the preface to *Nick of the Woods* by Robert Montgomery Bird (1837)

Sample Question 5

(Suggested time: 40 minutes. This question counts for one-third of the total essay section score.)

The following essay, "Stranded in Suburbia," was written by Paul Krugman, Princeton professor, economist, and regular editorialist for *The New York Times*. Read the passage carefully. Then write an essay in which you analyze the strategies Krugman uses to develop a position on suburban living and the American way of life.

I have seen the future, and it works.°

O.K., I know that these days you're supposed to see the future in China or India, not in the heart of "old Europe."

5   But we're living in a world in which oil prices keep setting records, in which the idea that global oil production will soon peak is rapidly moving from fringe belief to mainstream assumption. And Europeans who have achieved a high standard of living in spite of very high energy prices—gas in Germany costs more than $8 a gallon—have a lot to teach us about how to deal with that world.

10 If Europe's example is any guide, here are the two secrets of coping with expensive oil: own fuel-efficient cars, and don't drive them too much.

Notice that I said that cars should be fuel-efficient—not that people should do without cars altogether. In Germany, as in the United States, the vast majority of families own cars (although German households are less likely

15 than their U.S. counterparts to be multiple-car owners).

But the average German car uses about a quarter less gas per mile than the average American car. By and large, the Germans don't drive itsy-bitsy toy cars, but they do drive modest-sized passenger vehicles rather than S.U.V.'s and pickup trucks.

20 In the near future I expect we'll see Americans moving down the same path. We've already done it once: over the course of the 1970s and 1980s, the average mileage of U.S. passenger vehicles rose about 50 percent, as Americans switched to smaller, lighter cars.

This improvement stalled with the rise of S.U.V.'s during the cheapgas

25 1990s. But now that gas costs more than ever before, even after adjusting for inflation, we can expect to see mileage rise again.

Admittedly, the next few years will be rough for families who bought big vehicles when gas was cheap, and now find themselves the owners of white elephants with little trade-in value. But raising fuel efficiency is something we

30 can and will do.

Can we also drive less? Yes—but getting there will be a lot harder.

I have seen . . . it works: Krugman quotes the famous comment made by American muckraking journalist Lincoln Steffens (1866–1936) after a visit to the Soviet Union in 1919.

There have been many news stories in recent weeks about Americans who are changing their behavior in response to expensive gasoline—they're trying to shop locally, they're canceling vacations that involve a lot of driving, and they're switching to public transit.

But none of it amounts to much. For example, some major public transit systems are excited about ridership gains of 5 or 10 percent. But fewer than 5 percent of Americans take public transit to work, so this surge of riders takes only a relative handful of drivers off the road.

Any serious reduction in American driving will require more than this—it will mean changing how and where many of us live.

To see what I'm talking about, consider where I am at the moment: in a pleasant, middle-class neighborhood consisting mainly of four- or five-story apartment buildings, with easy access to public transit and plenty of local shopping.

It's the kind of neighborhood in which people don't have to drive a lot, but it's also a kind of neighborhood that barely exists in America, even in big metropolitan areas. Greater Atlanta has roughly the same population as Greater Berlin—but Berlin is a city of trains, buses and bikes, while Atlanta is a city of cars, cars and cars.

And in the face of rising oil prices, which have left many Americans stranded in suburbia—utterly dependent on their cars, yet having a hard time affording gas—it's starting to look as if Berlin had the better idea.

Changing the geography of American metropolitan areas will be hard. For one thing, houses last a lot longer than cars. Long after today's S.U.V.'s have become antique collectors' items, millions of people will still be living in subdivisions built when gas was $1.50 or less a gallon.

Infrastructure is another problem. Public transit, in particular, faces a chicken-and-egg problem: it's hard to justify transit systems unless there's sufficient population density, yet it's hard to persuade people to live in denser neighborhoods unless they come with the advantage of transit access.

And there are, as always in America, the issues of race and class. Despite the gentrification° that has taken place in some inner cities, and the plunge in national crime rates to levels not seen in decades, it will be hard to shake the longstanding American association of higher-density living with poverty and personal danger.

Still, if we're heading for a prolonged era of scarce, expensive oil, Americans will face increasingly strong incentives to start living like Europeans—maybe not today, and maybe not tomorrow, but soon, and for the rest of our lives.

[2008]

---

gentrification: restoration of poor urban areas by well-to-do new homeowners, leading to displacement of the original inhabitants

Analysis Prompts
Answers and Explanations

ANSWER AND EXPLANATION

Analysis Prompt: Malcolm Gladwell
"Small Change, Why the Revolution Will Not Be Tweeted"

A successful essay will effectively communicate Gladwell's argument, which articulates that the new social media lacks the "discipline and strategy" to have any lasting or significant impact on society. While the author employs a number of strategies, the most effective one is his refutation to "the bible of the social-media movement," Clay Shirky's "Here Comes Everybody." While Gladwell concedes the example of "an army of people" tracking down a cell phone has its merits—"this is the kind of thing that could never have happened in the pre-Internet era"—he argues that Shirky's "mode of activism" is "trivial" and "favors [only] weak-tie connections." This position allows Gladwell to develop his contrast to the Shirky example: Martin Luther King's boycotts in the civil rights era of the 1950s and 60s. Gladwell argues King's followers had to "persevere in the face of danger," which is not required by activists utilizing social networks requiring only "weak-tie connections" and using instruments that are not necessarily "natural enem[ies] of the status quo." Finally, excellent responses will identify Gladwell's use of understatement at the conclusion of the excerpt. Here, Gladwell's response to Shirky's portentous question—"What happens next?"—is a pithy "*Viva la revolución*," punctuating Gladwell's argument that real social change requires more than "helping Wall Streeters get phones back from teen-age girls."

ANSWER AND EXPLANATION

Analysis Prompt: Ralph Waldo Emerson
"Nature"

Excellent responses to this prompt will clearly articulate the truth that is revealed through nature and the process of personal introspection as proposed by Emerson. Numerous rhetorical strategies and devices are employed throughout the excerpt. However, the most notable are Emerson's use of parallelism, questioning, imagery, and metaphor. Lines such as "there are new lands, new men, new thoughts" utilize parallelism to promote the premise of forging new and unique experiences with the natural world. Additionally, the questions posed in the first paragraph beg the reader to engage with Emerson's argument to consider how meaning and revelation are provoked. The striking imagery strives to evoke the natural world for the reader. Most importantly, however, excellent responses will demonstrate a strong understanding of Emerson's philosophical argument.

ANSWER AND EXPLANATION

Analysis Prompt: John Okada
No-No Boy

The excellent essay will focus on the immediate shift in the way that Japanese Americans were perceived by various segments of the American population. The first two paragraphs focus on the immediacy of this shift in perception, an immediacy brought on by the Japanese attack on Pearl Harbor. The author's repeated reference to "the moment" highlights this, as does his reference to the perception that the Japanese were now "animals of a different breed." Additionally, the excellent essay will note the impact of this shift in the subsequent paragraphs on citizens as varied as a college professor, a town drunk, and a salesman. The college professor, despite his erudite background, fails to impart any wisdom on the situation; the town drunk turns against his Japanese-American landlord, despite his kind and generous nature; and the salesman uses the event to confirm his unsubstantiated suspicions about his Japanese-American client's business acumen. Ultimately, however, what governs this passage are the references to the media, such as the one found in the final line: "The radio said as much." These references suggest that the shifts in public perception had been sparked and promoted by a media that had demonized all Japanese Americans for the events of December 7, 1941.

ANSWER AND EXPLANATION

Analysis Prompt: George Catlin and Robert Montgomery Bird
Views of American Indians

A successful essay will clearly delineate the two distinct attitudes conveyed in the Catlin and Bird excerpts. Further, a highly competent essay will make note of the various rhetorical strategies used by the two authors to further their points of view. Both writers utilize Western traditions to draw upon their readers' pre-existing knowledge to more clearly communicate their respective points of view. Catlin compares American Indians to Greek Olympians and chivalrous knights of the medieval tradition, while Bird references shepherds of the pastoral school of poetry. However, while Catlin draws a traditional comparison to evoke his sense of respect and reverence for the American Indians, Bird manipulates the traditional view of the pastoral shepherd as a Romantic figure, pointing out the true state of a shepherd—far more ragged and uncivilized than the romanticized version. His American Indians are marked not by athletic prowess and noble virtues, but by dirty shirts and barbarism. Beyond the allusions mentioned above, both excerpts make use of description and imagery to enhance their presentations of their own views of American Indians.

ANSWER AND EXPLANATION

Analysis Prompt: Paul Krugman
"Stranded in Suburbia"

Excellent responses to the Krugman essay will focus on a number of rhetorical strategies and decisions. One involves Krugman's persona. Despite his credentials as a Princeton professor and leading economist, Krugman addresses a broad audience, referencing famous quotations from muckraking journalists and lines from popular American cinema. His diction selection is also directed toward a broader audience, using such terms as "stalled" and "cheap" to impart an informal relationship with his audience. The resulting effect helps to demystify Krugman's elevated professional position in academia. Excellent responses will also notice Krugman's use of comparison: American gas prices to European gas prices, American cities to German cities, and American driving habits to German diving habits. Such comparisons help to support Krugman's claims that in order to address the problems sparked by a "prolonged era of scarce, expensive oil," Americans need to consider the ways in which other nations are tackling similar issues. Additionally, excellent responses will note Krugman's use of anecdotal evidence, such as the references to "many news stories ... about Americans who are trying to change their behavior." Krugman ultimately juxtaposes this anecdotal evidence in the following paragraph, when he examines hard data that suggest "fewer than 5 percent of Americans take public transit to work," essentially refuting the anecdotal evidence presented in the previous paragraph. Finally, excellent responses will note the hurdles Krugman documents at the end. While he does not propose solutions, he acknowledges the hurdles and, more importantly, the degree to which they will continue to dominate discussions about suburban living and the American way of life well into the future.

Argument Essay

Introduction

The argument prompt is, like the other two writing prompts, fairly formulaic in its construction. You will undoubtedly be provided with either a short quote or claim that makes an assertion about a topic. You task is to consider the claim and either defend, challenge, or qualify its assertion. If you choose to defend the claim, you will provide evidence that best supports your position. If you choose to challenge the claim, you will provide an opposing argument, complete with evidence to support your counterargument. If you choose to qualify the claim—which can be a difficult task but one that has the potential to provoke a more thoughtful, nuanced response—you will consider the circumstances under which you can agree with the claim and those circumstances in which you challenge it. The danger, of course, in qualifying an argument is that the writer fails to take any position on the issue at all and, instead, appears indecisive. Still, if you can avoid vacillating on the topic and articulate those situations in which you can defend the claim, this approach may bear more fruit than simply defending or challenging the position. Ultimately, you must arrive at a position in which your convictions are apparent and your logic sound.

Approaching the Argument Prompt

Before responding to the argument prompt, it is critical that you first unpack its language carefully. Be sure to underline key words or phrases, terms that you will confront, repeat, and reuse in your own response. Make sure you understand the quote or claim introducing the issue at hand, as a misunderstanding of the issue will prevent you from organizing and composing a successful essay. In fact, many well-written essays—that is, in terms of expression—often fail to score in the upper half as a result of a misinterpretation of the prompt itself. Don't fall into this pitfall.

Once you have unpacked the prompt, you should begin to consider evidence you might use to support your claim. Evidence should be specific and exact. It should demonstrate a broad understanding and command of the issue, and should seek to reflect a well-read, well-educated, and thoughtful mind. Avoid the temptation to use examples from movies, television shows, popular music or fiction, as they often reflect a narrow, immature view of the world. Consider, instead, examples from your studies, history, current events, the political realm, the world of literature, or anecdote that offer keen and mature insight into an issue. Don't, however, jump to conclusions. Use your time wisely and consider all sides of the issue before moving forward.

Perhaps the best strategy in collecting and organizing evidence in support of a claim is to create a two-columned T-chart. In one column you will list evidence in support of the claim, and in the other, you will list evidence that challenges that claim. Be sure to list as many examples as you can, so you can take a position that is well supported, and also so that you can consider ways in which you will refute the opposing viewpoints.

Organizing and Composing Your Argumentative Essay

It is suggested that you follow the organizing principles of the classical model as discussed in the synthesis section of this same guide. You should, in the essay's introduction, clearly state your position and, ideally, provide your audience with a roadmap for your argument. You might consider beginning your essay with an analogy or some other type of hook device, but avoid spending too much time composing an ornate or complex opening statement. Students often spend too much precious time beginning an essay and then fail to adequately support their position. If you cannot come up with a hook concept in a couple of minutes, move on and present your thesis.

When crafting your thesis, be sure to include key words from the prompt. This is a clear signal to readers that you have understood what is being asked of you. It is also important that you take a clear position on the issue being presented and that you use strong diction to express this position. Eliminate phrases such as "I feel" or "I think" from your thesis; they weaken the strength of your argument. You should maintain a strong voice throughout your essay.

The following paragraphs, the body of your essay, should present your evidence. It is important that you include ample, strong evidence to support your position. The quality and quantity of your support pieces are critical to proving your point to your audience. Several pieces of support that are unclear or not directly related to your main point are just as likely to weaken your position as too few examples. It is extremely important that you establish how each example supports your position. It is your job as the author to clarify for the reader how each and every piece of evidence is tied to your claim. Again, maintain an authoritative voice as you build the support for your argument.

It is also advised that you build up to your strongest points in the body paragraphs. Your strongest pieces of support should come towards the essay's conclusion, leaving them fresh in your reader's mind.

All good arguments seek to address and, if possible, refute opposing positions. It is critical that you address potential refutations of your own position. This may be done either in the body of your essay, by anticipating and disproving objections to each piece of your evidence after you have presented it, or in the final body paragraph, wherein you may address all potential objections. Remember that even if you cannot disprove other viewpoints, it is important to address them and establish why your position is a stronger one.

The conclusion is, perhaps, the most important part of your argument essay. Too often, students simply content themselves with restating their position in a terse, short concluding paragraph. If time is running out, you should undoubtedly do the same. However, if you manage your time properly, you can use the conclusion as an opportunity to further engage your audience in the cause. This final appeal goes beyond the mere acknowledgment of your logic as presented in your essay and asks your audience to act upon your suggestions.

Sample Argument Essays

Sample Question 1

(Suggested time: 40 minutes. This question counts for one-third of the total essay section score.)

H.W. Fowler, teacher, lexicographer, and author of multiple books on language and usage, commented in his book *The King's English* (1908) on the use of slang in both written and oral communication. He said:

> To the ordinary man, of average intelligence and middle-class position, slang comes from every direction, from above, from below, and from all sides, as well as from the centre. What comes from some directions he will know for slang, what comes from others he may not. He may be expected to
> 5   recognize words from below. Some of these are shortenings, by the lower classes, of words whose full form conveys no clear meaning, and is therefore useless, to them. An antiquated example is *mob,* for *mobile vulgus.* That was once slang, and is now good English. A modern one is *bike,* which will very likely be good English also in time. But though its brevity is a strong recom-
> 10   mendation, and its uncouthness probably no more than subjective and transitory, it is as yet slang. Such words should not be used in print till they have become so familiar that there is not the slightest temptation to dress them up in quotation marks. Though they are the most easily detected, they are also the best slang; when the time comes, they take their place in
> 15   the language as words that will last, and not, like many of the more highly descended words, die away uselessly after a brief popularity.

> —from Fowler's *The Kings English*, 2nd Edition (1908)

With the ubiquitous nature of technology, communications, blogs, and social media, language is rapidly evolving, and slang is used more often in written communications—even formal written communications—than it, perhaps, has ever been used before. In a well-written essay, develop a position on the appropriateness of using slang in written communication. Support your position with evidence from your readings, observations, and/or experiences.

Sample Question 2

(Suggested time: 40 minutes. This question counts for one-third of the total essay section score.)

Henry David Thoreau often commented on the manipulative nature of a consumer culture. In such a culture, average citizens are encouraged to buy luxuries and replace functional goods with those that are newer and improved regardless of need or financial ability. In the chapter "Economy" from *Walden,* Thoreau wrote

> . . . the childish and savage taste of men and women for new patterns keeps how many shaking and squinting through kaleidoscopes that they may discover the particular figure which this generation requires today. The manufacturers have learned that this taste is merely whimsical.
>
> —from *Walden* by Thoreau

Think about the implications of a culture built on consumption. Then write an essay that develops a position on the relative value of a consumer-driven culture and its influence on the health and prosperity of a nation.

Sample Question 3

(Suggested time: 40 minutes. This question counts for one-third of the total essay section score.)

Lao Tzu, a sixth-century B.C. Chinese philosopher, once said: "A leader is best when people barely know he exists; when his work is done, his aim fulfilled, they will say: we did it ourselves. "

Consider this quotation about leadership. Then write an essay that defends, challenges or qualifies Lao Tzu's assertion about the "best" quality of a leader. Support your argument with appropriate evidence from your readings, observations, or experiences.

Sample Question 4

(Suggested time: 40 minutes. This question counts for one-third of the total essay section score.)

In his essay "Self-Reliance," Ralph Waldo Emerson claims,

> "There is a time in every man's education when he arrives at the conviction that envy is ignorance; that imitation is suicide; that he must take himself for better, for worse, as his portion; that though the wide universe is full of good, no kernel of nourishing corn can come to him but through his toil bestowed on that plot of ground which is given to him to till."

Consider Emerson's observation. Then write an essay that defends, challenges, or qualifies the author's belief that a true understanding of one's own nature and purpose in life can only come about as the result of hard work and self-reliance.

Sample Question 5

(Suggested time: 40 minutes. This question counts for one-third of the total essay section score.)

In an 1822 letter, James Madison wrote of the importance of education in providing for the preservation and continuity of a free and democratic state. The letter, provoked by a debate regarding taxation and the funding of public institutions of learning in Kentucky, argues both for the benefits of a learned citizenry and the necessity of those more fortunate to help fund schools and institutions of higher learning. Read the following passage. Then develop a position on the responsibility of those more fortunate to contribute to the education and advancement of those less fortunate.

> But why should it be necessary in this case, to distinguish the Society into classes according to their property? When it is considered that the establishment and endowment of Academies, Colleges, and Universities are a provision, not merely for the existing generation, but for succeeding ones also; that
> 5   in Governments like ours a constant rotation of property results from the free scope to industry, and from the laws of inheritance, and when it is considered moreover, how much of the exertions and privations of all are meant not for themselves, but for their posterity, there can be little ground for objections from any class, to plans of which every class must have its turn of benefits.
> 10   The rich man, when contributing to a permanent plan for the education of the poor, ought to reflect that he is providing for that of his own descendants; and the poor man who concurs in a provision for those who are not poor that at no distant day it may be enjoyed by descendants from himself. It does not require a long life to witness these vicissitudes of fortune.
>
>   —*The Writing of James Madison.* Edited by Gaillard Hunt.
>   9 vols. New York: G. P. Putnam's Sons, 1900–1910.

Scoring and Student Samples

The AP® Scoring Rubric

The following rubric is similar to those used to score the AP® exam. The rubric has been adapted for use of the first argument prompt on slang, found on page 115 of this book.

9: These essays offer a **highly effective and nuanced** argument on the appropriateness of using slang in written communication. The student provides examples and evidence that are apt and highly persuasive, and the argument is extremely articulate and well-developed. The written expression demonstrates the student's ability to project a convincing voice and to consistently control a wide range of the elements of effective writing. However, given the time constraints, these essays need not be flawless.

8: These essays, while still **effective and nuanced**, offer a slightly less sophisticated or nuanced argument than those scoring a 9. Still, these essays represent a perceptive response to the prompt and a well-reasoned and rigorous argument.

7: These essays offer a **thoughtful argument** on the appropriateness of using slang in written communication. Students who compose an essay earning a score of 7 meet the criteria for a score of 6, but they give a more complete explanation, provide more thorough development, or compose in more mature prose style. However, these essays tend to be more formulaic than those scoring in the upper tier; they may rely on less persuasive evidence, or may lack the sophisticated voice and written expression found in upper tier essays.

6: These essays offer an **adequate argument** on the appropriateness of using slang in written communication. However, the evidence and explanations used are marked by a weaker argument and a less confident expression. Still, these essays respond to the prompt adequately and support their claims sufficiently.

5: These essays present a **plausible argument** on the appropriateness of using slang in written communication. However, the evidence or explanations used may be poorly balanced, limited, or inadequately developed. Rather than a well-developed presentation of evidence, the writing may offer examples but without adequate explanation. The writing may contain lapses in diction or syntax, but it usually conveys the student's ideas without too much work on the reader's part.

4: These essays **inadequately** develop a position on the appropriateness of using slang in written communication. They approach the task too simply or inaccurately. The evidence or explanations used may be inappropriate, undeveloped, or less convincing. The writing and logic may be repetitive and marred by surface errors.

3: Essays earning a score of 3 approach the task **too simply or inadequately**. They meet the criteria for a score of 4, but demonstrate even less success in developing a position on the appropriateness of using slang in written communication. The evidence may be slight, unconvincing, or over-simplistic. The essays may also demonstrate less maturity with regard to grammar, usage, and mechanics.

2: The essays reveal only a **perfunctory** attempt to answer the prompt and offer little grasp of the task at hand. These essays may only partially understand the prompt or offer evidence that is only tangentially related to the topic at hand. The argument is flawed in all areas of evidence, organization and expression.

1: These essays reflect even less ability with expression and the basic tenets of argument.

0: Indicates some response was made, but one that warrants no credit.

__ Indicates a blank response.

Sample Student Essays

SAMPLE 1

All expressions of culture, no matter how stagnant and non-changing they may seem in the moment, are constantly evolving so as not to fall behind with the extreme speed that technology is introduced, discoveries are made, and popular styles are changed throughout the years. This metamorphosis applies to events as mundane as the style of eyeglass lenses over the decades, or as significant as the status of nations as they are affected by war, politics, and global economy. The written and spoken word, the common thread that unites all aspects of culture, and provides a language in which customs can be reviewed and discussed, undergoes this evolution as well. As British lexicographer H.W. Fowler discussed in the turn of the twentieth century, slang is an integral part of this language development; many new words or phrases are introduced as informal slang, and, throughout the decades, rise the lexicographic ladder until they are on the level with the most basic of words in the language, all memory of their slang roots forgotten. Therefore, slang is a necessary part of speech, showing how the language has evolved over time due to influence from new events and social groups. This sect of vocabulary is also useful, especially in written communication, to differentiate between different groups to whom a person is appealing the subject he is discussing, and in the medium of writing employed. Therefore, slang is a necessary part of speech, but must be regulated according to the setting.

The primary use of slang in writing is to appeal to a certain group or audience. Usually, the more familiar the person receiving the piece of writing is to the writer, the more slang that may be exchanged without fear of offence or the recipient lowering his opinion of the writer. This reveals that the use of slang is closely linked to a level of respect; the more credentials the writer wants to reveal to his reader, and the more respect he wants to foster, the less slang will be used. Therefore, between close friends who have already established a high opinion of each other, the use of slang will not greatly affect their relationship. However, in a setting where it is important to foster respect for the writer, it is important that slang not be used. In situations such as college essays, where the student desires to be viewed positively by the admissions director of the school, the student should use formal language to both show his ability to use Standard Written English to express an idea, and also his ability to curb his vocabulary for what is appropriate in the setting. However, just as it is important to employ a certain type of speech to heighten a person's perceived intelligence, there are also situations where a person may need to adopt a less refined level of speech to appeal to a group that is less educated. The manner in which a teacher writes a note to her first-grade student would use a different set of vocabulary, one that the child would understand, as opposed to a letter addressed to the child's mother, which would use language similar to the teacher's own. Therefore, the audience receiving the written communication is a great teller of the amount of slang that may be used.

Aside from the group reading the work, the subject matter of the piece can also determine the type of vocabulary that is proper to use. Works of fiction are generally less formal, and therefore may include more slang than a piece of non-fiction writing that is more concerned with factual information rather than conveying a certain voice. Along these lines, a novel describing the day-to-day life of a character would probably use language and slang that the character would use and hear in his daily life. Therefore, the vocabulary is used as a literary device, just like metaphor or personification, to allow the reader to delve into the novel's world. On the contrary, an article in a science journal would use little to no slang in communicating its hypothesis, and would follow a strict set of formal vocabulary known to fellow scientists and those reading the report. In this sense, just as social media words are the slang of teenagers, Latin-based technical terms are in many ways the slang of scientists: a special set of words used only to communicate to their group of peers about a certain subject. However, were the physicist to use this language outside of the lab to discuss subjects other than science, just as if the teenager were to use "text speak" to discuss the themes of a poem in his English class, his method of communication would not be effective, because he was neither appealing to his audience nor using language that fit the subject matter at hand.

Finally, the medium of written communication shows the level of appropriate slang that may be used. With the rise of computer technology and social media, email and messaging have replaced quick, hand-written notes as the least formal forms of writing. Texts and messages on social media websites are plagued with abbreviated words, acronyms, and a dearth of punctuation to make the speed of communication as quick as possible. Email, while usually possessing proper spelling and capitalization, is still a less formal means of communication than a typed or hand-written letter sent through the mail system. However, this is becoming less true as many colleagues in the workplace communicate less though mail and telephone, and more through the Internet. The means of writing to determine slang does not only apply to correspondence; books and periodicals are also forms of writing that require a certain level of either formality or informality. A graphic novel, because of the inclusion of pictures that makes it similar to a comic, would possess more slang than a larger novel, and even more than a work of non-fiction that is used to educate, rather than entertain.

Slang and the introduction of new words into speech and writing are necessary and even welcomed by many as a token that the language, along with society and the customs of people employing the language, is changing. Words were introduced in the time of William Shakespeare that seemed laughable and perhaps even rude at the time, such as gloomy, the adjective of the noun gloom, or worthless, which is merely enjambment of two separate words to create a new one. However, they have been used so often in the language that they now occupy a place in the Standard Written English dictionary, and are no longer considered slang. However, just as a seventeenth-century student would never remark to his professor about the gloomy weather outside, contemporary speakers must keep in mind the audience and subject matter they are conveying to determine which words would be considered inappropriate or slang in the situation.

SAMPLE 2

Words are tools for success. They unlock jobs, create opportunities, and, most importantly, allow essential communication both verbal and written. Words are also constantly evolving; new phrases, terms, and forms of slang go in and out of fashion as quickly as the modern world can broadcast them. The proper use of words, slang or otherwise, is therefore impossible to define. In written communication, the words used depend upon the intended outcome and recipient of the document. Therefore, slang use in writing is as appropriate as the purpose of the message allows.

The use of slang or informal language in writing is only appropriate if the words correspond to the intended outcome of the work. The word choices made to greet a friend in an email, for example, would not be the same ones used to solicit a donation from a respected organization in a letter. The word choice in a written document must agree and balance with the level of language commonly used for the purpose of the letter in order to be appropriate. One could argue that whether or not a word is slang or informal language depends entirely upon the context it is used in. The status of any word as 'slang' is based on human perception and acceptance of that word into the standard vocabulary. Therefore, a written word only becomes recognizable as slang when it does not blend in with the level of language expected by its audience. If a politician received a letter with the heading, "what's up, man?" the letter would be thrown in the trash because of its blatant informal rudeness, however, the word choices simply do not match the accepted language of the target audience. If a child wrote to his grandparents with the opening, "Dear Sir and Madam," the same is true. In other words, written slang is only appropriate within its accepted community, in which case it can no longer be called slang by anyone but an outsider.

However, in some instances, slang is appropriate outside of its accepted community when used as a rhetorical strategy. This concept can be thought of as a written colloquialism, an attempt to connect with those of a different group by using their slang or vernacular. In the sixteenth century, Martin Luther translated religious works into the German peasant vernacular from Latin, the elevated language of the time. He reached many more people by writing this way. The German slang he used didn't seem out of place because it fit the audience receiving the document and furthered the intended outcome of the message, which was to allow the common people to read religious texts directly. Into the twenty-first century, everyone from politicians to children uses the idea of writing with the slang dialect of a different group to gain inclusion or connect with that audience. A friend staying with a host family in London, for example, wrote letters to them, and used the British terms: "telly" and "flat". Her way of integrating herself into that word community was subtler than a white male from Vermont writing "YO!" on a social networking site, but both used slang terms, or words foreign to the outsider in that community, to reach an audience, and convey the purpose behind the words, just as Martin Luther reached his audience with a new translation.

The appropriateness of slang usage in written communication depends on the intended recipient and purpose of the document. These words form a 'language' that belongs to a specific community of writers or people who identify with the slang. This slang or wording written to someone outside the language group results in a label of inappropriate language use, while it is really a question of the two sides being mutually incompatible. Because of the evolving nature of language and its dependence upon social groups, written slang is only acceptable if the intended outcome and the recipient of the message justify its use.

SAMPLE 3

The use and appropriateness of slang has long been debated. In 1908, H.W. Fowler, a lexicographer, discussed slang in *The King's English*, one of his multiple books on language and usage, stating that he believed slang words "should not be used in print" until their familiarity had reached the level that there was "not the slightest temptation to dress them up in quotation marks." This quote also shows a common view on current slang: that it needs to be dressed up, made to look more formal, before it can successfully enter written communication. In current American society, the age of modern technology and the subsequent rise of blogs and social media has allowed language to develop more rapidly than, perhaps, ever before. This has led to a heightened conflict over the appropriateness of slang in written communication. Although the development of language over time allows certain slang to eventually become good English, modern slang should not be used in formal written communication, such as schoolwork or scholarly articles, because word choice should depend on the discourse community being addressed.

The current debate over the use and appropriateness of slang in written communication is analyzed in David Foster Wallace's essay *Tense Present* in Harper's Magazine, in which he described the ongoing battle between so-called descriptivists, who believe that all ways of expressing oneself through writing are equal regardless of adherence to the rules of grammar, and prescriptivists, who strictly and stubbornly follow the rules of grammar and do not accept deviation from the aforementioned rules. Descriptivists will accept the use of slang in writing because they see it as a way of expressing oneself. Since language develops over time, current slang will, for the most part, eventually be considered "good English" that is appropriate for writing. However, modern slang is not appropriate for formal written communication. Often crude, vulgar, and grammatically incorrect, it can make the writer appear incredibly unintelligent. While a descriptivist approach to written communication might be acceptable when posting on facebook or twitter, it is best to follow a more prescriptivist approach in formal writing by avoiding slang.

Finally, slang is inappropriate for formal writing because written communication must be compiled with the desired audience in mind. While it might be perfectly appropriate to use slang in written communication with friends, peers, or certain family members, it is not appropriate to use slang in formal writing, such as schoolwork, or letters, partly because members this particular discourse community will not only be unlikely to use slang themselves, but also because they will probably not take the writer seriously, as using slang reflects poorly on their educational level and abilities. For example, if a high school student were to write a paper that evaluated one situation as "cool," or used exclamations such as, "this sucks!," their grade would be marked down unless their teacher happened to be an ardent descriptivist, which is highly unlikely. Another issue is that many current slang words, such as "emo," could be considered offensive. The writer must have the intended audience in mind and act accordingly. Modern slang, while potentially appropriate for written communications with friends or peers, is not suited for formal writing.

The rise of social media and blogs through the rapid improvement of technology has facilitated the rapid evolving of the English language, with the result that the debate over the appropriateness of slangs in written communications has intensified. Slang should not be used in formal written communications, such as scholarly articles, for several reasons. First of all, use of slang in formal writing reduces the credibility of the author by causing them to appear less intelligent. Also, since the intended audience must be considered when writing, and those who read formal writing tend to belong to a different discourse community than those who commonly use slang, it is best to avoid using these terms in formal written communication. Many slang words could also be viewed as offensive or politically incorrect. In short, while slang may be suitable for written communication with friends, peers, or certain family members, it is not fitting for formal writing, because, in the eyes of many who read formal written work, all forms of written communication are not equal.

SAMPLE 4

In day-to-day life, one confronts the English language in a variety of ways. From writing edited reports for class to leaving quick notes on the counter for a family member, the levels of professionalism we utilize in language every day are many. The focus on elevated language skills, such as good grammar and vocabulary, are prevalent in English classes. Along with those, it is important to take slang into consideration when writing a piece of written communication, because it can help or hinder an argument when making a point. Like H. W. Fowler wrote in his book *The King's English (1908)* ". . . such words should not be used in print 'till they have become so familiar that there is not the slightest temptation to dress them up in quotation marks." As a general rule, one should refrain from using slang when writing a professional argument. However, when using language on blogs and social media, less formal forms of communication, slang is an acceptable form of delivering a point across.

Slang words are not part of Standard English. They are considered informal. Throughout history, the use of proper language has forever been a sign of intelligence and respect. For example, when Shakespeare intended to make one appear less intelligent, he used that time period's slang in their dialogue. "The word "bench-whistler," for instance, was a lethargic person who never finished his work. As many of us are unfamiliar with the word "bench-whistler," it is important to add that slang words usually die from the language after a short period of time, never become acceptable to Standard English. As H.W. Fowler said, slang "die(s) away uselessly after a brief popularity. When one uses informal writing in written communication, the audience will be less receptive to the author who appears unwise. When writing a letter to a professor, for example, one would not begin by writing: "Hey bro! It's been a while since we've chatted! What's up dawg?" If such an instance were to occur, the professor would be disappointed, insulted, and not at all receptive. Slang has no place in formal communication.

Undoubtedly, slang does have a place in daily life. For example, when one uses slang to tell jokes to friends through social media, they would not be mocked for their informal usage. A similar interaction occurs in person. In fact, it could potentially be a bit odd if your best friend were to say this when you parted: "Pardon me, dear comrade. May I be so delighted as to escort you to your vehicle?" One would most likely be confused and worried about their friend if the behavior continued. The ability to and know when different formalities are needed comes in handy. In informal circumstances with written communication with friends, it is acceptable to use slang. When in doubt, one would most likely be safer to not use slang in written communication. (Did you notice the use of the slang word, "handy"?)

Slang surrounds us wherever we go, and it is important to differentiate the situations in which it is acceptable to use, and when more formal language is necessary. If one continually uses slang in written communication, the outcomes for being viewed as an intelligent individual is not likely. However, if one consistently writes without slang in less formal situations, they will most likely be ridiculed for not understanding social cues. As a general rule, written communication should not imply slang, unless one is positive it will be the most acceptable way of interacting.

SAMPLE 5

Standard Written English, the official language of the English written world, changes slowly in reply to the changes in spoken English. With the advances in technology, however, the once formal letter has been replaced with the faster, more informal email. Telephone conversations are nearly extinct among the world of young adults, replaced with texts and other instant messaging. With the broader spectrum of uses for the written language, written language will adapt faster to small changes, bringing modern slang into even formal writing. The use of slang and other informal language, when used well, can create an increased sense of audience that appeals to the reader, without obstructing understanding, while it also lessens credibility.

The audience of formal papers is vast, and different for each paper. When appealing to less educated people, for example, one might use more slang and less advanced diction. For instance, political campaigning offers a challenge to the candidates. They must be understandable to every person in the country, while still creating a professional, knowledgeable front. If a candidate used too advanced diction, some people would decide the candidate knew nothing about the average person; if they used only colloquial language, others would decide they were too simple, too common, to be in office. The use of slang, or even just informal speech, gives a connection between the speaker and the audience; if it did not, then formal writing would be used for everything.

The assumption that the use of the vernacular somehow makes a paper inherently wrong stems from education. Without this, every student would write the way he spoke. For school essays, for instance, I would avoid using 'I', because it's considered improper in formal papers, according to Standard Written English. Contractions, also, are avoided. Every student would avoid these words, because it is taught in school to use Standard Written English every time, everywhere, with everyone. This, however, gives the false assumption that it is somehow wrong to use colloquialisms in formal language. The use of the first person pronoun often assists in giving the paper a personal touch. It relates a broad subject to the life of an individual, and if it touches one person's life, why can't it touch the reader's, too? In many cases, the use of the personal pronoun could add more than it detracts; it is only avoided because of the difficulty of creating one such case. But this continues to be taught to be wrong, because it lessens credibility. The use of the personal pronoun, to continue on that example, changes the facts from being from research, from the vast knowledge the world offers, to one person's perspective, and a student's, at that. Each paper stems from one person's knowledge, incapable of spanning a subject area well enough to discuss it intelligently, but the reader wants to believe that the author feeds him perfect and indisputable fact.

Nothing is inherently wrong with using slang in formal as well as informal writing. The use of slang, personal pronouns, or what is considered a grammar mistake, can sometimes add to the writing. The author must always be aware of the audience, and how to reach that audience. If slang is a viable method to connect with an audience, then it should be an acceptable option for the writer to take advantage of. All writing argues for one opinion, and while these opinions may be disguised to look like truth, slang may also advocate that opinion. An avoidance of slang in written communication on principle is nothing more than a self-imposed handicap.

SAMPLE 6

What's wrong with TV? This sentence would seem normal and grammatically correct to ninety percent of Americans. "what's" and "TV" are both examples of words that were once considered slang and are now technically words, don't believe me check the dictionary. Because these words became so popular they stuck," and not, like many of the more highly descended words, die away uselessly after brief popularity" as Fowler mentioned. Although many slang words make it much more convenient to send a text and get things written faster, too much slang is not appropriate in written English.

The simplicity of the English language increases every single day, even I can admit to slaughtering a sentence with far too many words such as "like" or "dude". The word dude is usually only used in spoken language, but because it is said so much upcoming generations who are influenced by what adults say are putting these words into their writing. These slang words are starting to appear in written English more and more with each generation. The English language from the eighteen hundreds and the English language now show the increase of the butchered language, English is no longer as eloquent as it once was. Even a person with a master's in English literature has done it, used slang in spoken as well as written English. The old form of more proper English should be preserved.

The use of certain slang words can be useful; they can cut the amount of words used in a sentence, and in some groups are preferred over the proper use of diction. To use the proper word among certain groups may seem odd, so by using slang one could possibly fit into a desired group. Using slang can seem great in this way but this can't keep getting worse, this regurgitating of our language. Even if thought to be odd for using proper diction, those people must stand up and help preserve the more eloquent English. If people do not correct each other and stand up one day all we will hear is sentences such as "dude, like, do you wanna go like to the um. . . . rad thingy now", which one day is what our written English will sound like if we don't fix this problem.

We have all done it; we have all used slang and not cared or even thought about correcting ourselves. Even an AP® English teacher has been caught using slang that just diffuses the effectiveness of his sentences. It's not just skate-boarders that use slang (which is what you thought of during my rad thingy sentence), but even the most educated of Americans use slang. Obviously slang will never be completely gone, because yes it can be convenient but it just can't drive the same point across that eloquent old English can, especially on paper. Old English must be preserved unless we want our future books, journals, essays and documents filled with ums, likes, dudes and bros.

SAMPLE 7

In this world, there is an abundance of technology and ways to communicate. There are written ways of communication, there are verbal ways of communication. People can text each other, people can call each other. It is incredible. Often times when people write each other they forget about the importance of proper formal language. Slang is too often used in incorrect situations. It is important to know when to use slang and when to not use slang in written language.

In informal situations, such as when you are texting or emailing your friend, using written communications, it has become normal for people to use slang. Words like "sup" and "yo" are thrown around continually, despite being politically incorrect. However, in these informal situations it is acceptable to use slang.

Despite there being numerous informal situations that now use written communication, there are still several formal situations that require formal language versus slang. For example, if you are writing a recommendation, you definitely don't want to use slang. It could prevent the person you are writing the recommendation for from appearing intelligent.

In the modern era, there are an incredible number of different situations using a variety of written ways of communication. Slang has become prominent in a large number of them. Despite there being situations where slang is acceptable, there are still plenty of formal situations when slang should not be used.

SAMPLE 8

When we communicate with other people, we give an impression of who we are. People judge us by what we say and how we say it. Slang, words that are informal and not correct English, can make people think badly of us when we use it in our writing.

Although slang is not appropriate in formal writing or speaking, it can work just fine in our daily lives. Our communications with our friends and family can be filled with slang and that is ok because the writing or speaking is informal. However, you cannot write to your boss or teacher using slang. It is not appropriate and creates a bad impression.

Slang is not really evil. It can be used for good as well. Slang will make a speaker or writer more approachable to an everyday audience. It could help create a voice people can connect with.

The trick is to know when it is safe to use slang, and when it is not.

SAMPLE 9

Slang is everywhere. You can't get into a conversation with talking some slang. Every time you say "yo dawg" it is slang. Slang can't be used in written communication.

Text messaging is pretty cool. You can message someone in a matter of minutes anything you want. It's ok for you to use slang then. If you want to say "Hey sup" to your friend there's nothing wrong with that.

However, you can't use slang when you write a text message to an important person. Your teacher doesn't want you to use "yo dawg" when you text them. They would prefer "Hello professor".

People are using slang too much in modern day language. It's kind of crazy and bad. They need to know when to use formal language.

Explanation of Scores

SAMPLE 1 – Score 9

This is a highly effective and nuanced essay, particularly given the time frame in which its author had to compose it. It offers an exhaustive argument that is well structured, well written, and logically sound. Additionally, it offers a wealth of apt examples as evidence, the majority of which are examined in great detail and depth. It offers an articulate argument, one that deeply explores the relationship between the writer and the audience. Additionally, it considers multiple forms of written communication, including the college essay, literature, poetry, and scientific writing. At its core is a nuanced understanding of the relationship between the audience and the author, and the importance of regulating one's language "according to the setting."

SAMPLE 2 – Score 8

While this essay is considerably shorter than its 9-scored counterpart, it still represents an effective and nuanced argument on the appropriateness of using slang in written communication. Its tidy opening paragraph wastes little time in clearly identifying the author's position, and the evidence provided in the body paragraphs are apt and demonstrate the author's rich understanding of the prompt. The well-developed references to Martin Luther and "German peasant vernacular" offer sophisticated evidence to support the author's position. Additionally, the author's sustained commentary on the relationship between the writer and audience is critical to its success. Although its analysis is strong and its writing is clear and succinct, it is not as rigorous or exhaustive in its examination of examples as its 9 counterpart.

SAMPLE 3 – Score 7

This thoughtful essay illustrates a good understanding of the prompt and offers a clear position on the topic at hand. Its reference to David Foster Wallace's work in the second paragraph is an especially apt one, one that demonstrates a sophisticated understanding of the history behind the "on-going battle between so-called descriptivists . . . and prescriptivists." The third paragraph offers a more pedestrian example, but the author's control of language and the rich and nuanced understanding of the topic make this an excellent example of a 7 essay. Had this author explored examples beyond the high school student's use of "cool" or "this sucks!" in the second body paragraph, this would have scored even higher.

SAMPLE 4 – Score 6

This essay begins well and offers a clear position on the topic at hand. The example in the first paragraph (Shakespeare's use of slang in his plays) is an apt one that leads into further discussion of the inappropriateness of using slang in formal communications with an authority figure—in this case a professor. The second body paragraph is less successful, as its example focuses more on oral communications between two friends, but the essay's conclusion returns to the prompt by clearly stating that language should be governed by one's targeted audience. Overall, this essay, while not without its flaws, offers an adequate response to the prompt.

SAMPLE 5 – Score 5

This essay offers a plausible—albeit too tangential—response to the topic at hand. It takes a position on the appropriateness of using slang in written communication and provides two examples to support its position. The first example examines the importance of balancing formal and informal language by politicians during political campaigns. While the example is an interesting one and not without merit, it unfortunately alludes to the use of informal language by politicians in oral communications and not written communications as the prompt directs. In this sense, the writer has strayed from the intent of the prompt. The second example, again while interesting, is limited in its ability to augment the author's argument. It focuses too much on the ways in which education has influenced the rules governing the use of personal pronouns. Overall, this essay offers some interesting insight, but its evidence is too tangential to the topic at hand.

SAMPLE 6 – Score 4

While this essay takes a position on the appropriateness of using slang in written communication, its evidence is overly simplistic and its expression is far too inform, which is ironic given the author's position on "proper English." The informal tone of the essay, the clumsy hook statement in the opening paragraph, and the repetitive logic of the essay are all indicators of an essay scoring in the lower half of the scoring. Still, the author takes a position and develops evidence—although in a limited sense.

SAMPLE 7 – Score 3

This essay approaches the task too simply and inadequately. While its four paragraphs provide a functional structure to its response, the examples provided lack depth and adequate discussion. Additionally, the writing has enough sentence errors and other mechanical flaws as to detract from a reader's understanding.

SAMPLE 8 – Score 2

While some attempt is made to address the prompt, the writer of this essay fails to develop any of the examples in a significant manner. The essay is too brief and undeveloped, and the examples cited in it do not demonstrate a rich understanding of the topic or the prompt.

SAMPLE 9 – Score 1

While some attempt is made by the author to address the prompt, the essay itself is perfunctory and immature, both in terms of expression and development. This essay is little more than a personal response regarding slang.

Section IV

Practice Exams

Questions 1–12. Read the following passage carefully before you select your answers.

(This passage is from a keynote address from a noted politician at the Democratic National Convention.)

Practice Exam A

Ten days ago, President Reagan admitted that although some people in this country seemed to be doing well nowadays, others were unhappy, even worried, about themselves, their families, and their futures. The President said that he didn't understand that fear. He said, "Why, this country is a shining city on a hill." And the President is right. In many ways we are a shining city on a hill.

But the hard truth is that not everyone is sharing in this city's splendor and glory. A shining city is perhaps all the President sees from the portico of the White House and the veranda of his ranch, where everyone seems to be doing well. But there's another city; there's another part to the shining city; the part where some people can't pay their mortgages, and most young people can't afford one; where students can't afford the education they need, and middle-class parents watch the dreams they hold for their children evaporate.

In this part of the city there are more poor than ever, more families in trouble, more and more people who need help but can't find it. Even worse: There are elderly people who tremble in the basements of the houses there. And there are people who sleep in the city streets, in the gutter, where the glitter doesn't show. There are ghettos where thousands of young people, without a job or an education, give their lives away to drug dealers every day. There is despair, Mr. President, in the faces that you don't see, in the places that you don't visit in your shining city.

In fact, Mr. President, this is a nation—Mr. President you ought to know that this nation is more a "Tale of Two Cities" than it is just a "Shining City on a Hill."

Maybe, maybe, Mr. President, if you visited some more places; maybe if you went to Appalachia where some people still live in sheds; maybe if you went to Lackawanna where thousands of unemployed steel workers wonder why we subsidized foreign steel.

Maybe—Maybe, Mr. President, if you stopped in at a shelter in Chicago and spoke to the homeless there; maybe, Mr. President, if you asked a woman who had been denied the help she needed to feed her children because you said you needed the money for a tax break for a millionaire or for a missile we couldn't afford to use.

Maybe—Maybe, Mr. President. But I'm afraid not. Because the truth is, ladies and gentlemen, that this is how we were warned it would be. President Reagan told us from the very beginning that he believed in a kind of social Darwinism. Survival of the fittest. "Government can't do everything," we were told, so it should settle for taking care of the strong and hope that economic ambition and charity will do the rest. Make the rich richer, and what falls from the table will be enough for the middle class and those who are trying desperately to work their way into the middle class.

You know, the Republicans called it "trickle-down" when Hoover tried it. Now they call it "supply side." But it's the same shining city for those relative few who are lucky enough to live in its good neighborhoods. But for the people who are excluded, for the people who are locked out, all they can do is stare from a distance at that city's glimmering towers.

It's an old story. It's as old as our history. The difference between Democrats and Republicans has always been measured in courage and confidence. The Republicans—The Republicans believe that the wagon train will not make it to the frontier unless some of the old, some of the young, some of the weak are left behind by the side of the trail. "The strong"—"The strong," they tell us, "will inherit the land."

We Democrats believe in something else. We Democrats believe that we can make it all the way with the whole family intact, and we have more than once. Ever since Franklin Roosevelt lifted himself from his wheelchair to lift this nation from its knees—wagon train after wagon train—to new frontiers of education, housing, peace; the whole family aboard, constantly reaching out to extend and enlarge that family; lifting them up into the wagon on the way; blacks and Hispanics, and people of every ethnic group, and native Americans—all those struggling to build their families and claim some small share of America. For nearly 50 years we carried them all to new levels of comfort, and security, and dignity, even affluence. And remember this, some of us in this room today are here only because this nation had that kind of confidence. And it would be wrong to forget that.

1. When read in the context of the entire speech, the speaker most likely introduces President Reagan at the start in order to
   (A) Pay tribute to the current President
   (B) Establish credibility by referencing a well-respected American
   (C) Attack Reagan's policies to control communism
   (D) Establish an adversarial figure for the rest of his speech
   (E) Push for more cooperation between the two political parties

2. Which of the following best characterizes the speaker's use of Reagan's "City on a Hill" quote in lines 7–8 throughout the rest of his speech?
   (A) He consistently agrees with the President on the greatness of America
   (B) He uses it to introduce a metaphor that will, when expanded, work against the President
   (C) He uses it to gain credibility by tying his speech back to the 1630 John Winthrop document of the same name
   (D) He uses it to emphasize the importance of New York City in the upcoming election
   (E) He uses it to criticize Reagan's handling of specific policies pertaining to New York City

3. In the sense that they are used to exemplify a broader lifestyle and worldview, the white house portico and ranch veranda mentioned in lines 13–14 are examples of:
   (A) Alliteration
   (B) Tautology
   (C) Ontology
   (D) Metonymy
   (E) Assonance

4. When he begins to discuss a different part of the city in the second and third paragraphs, the speaker is most likely
   (A) Outlining a plan for urban reform that can be implemented throughout the nation
   (B) Widening Reagan's metaphor to discuss the disadvantaged parts of the nation
   (C) Calling attention to the failure of social welfare programs
   (D) Arguing against entitlement programs already in place
   (E) Highlighting the fallacies in Reagan's earlier logic

5. Given the tone of the paragraph, the pronouns in lines 31–34 should best be read with:
   (A) Sadness
   (B) Sympathy
   (C) Bemusement
   (D) Sarcasm
   (E) Scorn

6. The paragraphs prefaced by the words "Maybe, Maybe, Mr. President" all rely on which of the following for their rhetorical affect?
   (A) Anecdote
   (B) Asymmetry
   (C) Apostrophe
   (D) Irony
   (E) Ellipses

7. The introduction of "A Tale of Two Cities" in line 37 is designed primarily to:
   (A) Attack Reagan for being a simple man who hasn't read many books
   (B) Provide a clever retort using another famous text
   (C) Warn of an impending revolution similar to that in Dickens's text
   (D) Demonstrate the speaker's erudite qualities to boost his ethos
   (E) Use a chiasmus to enliven his speech

8. The section of the speech from lines 39–65 contains which of the following literary devices?
   I. Anaphora
   II. Antanaclasis
   III. Metonymy

   (A) I and II only
   (B) II and III only
   (C) I and III only
   (D) I only
   (E) II only

9. In the context of the speech, the "wagon train" metaphor is an apt one to close with because it:
   (A) Shows an example where "trickle down" economics failed
   (B) Mocks Reagan for his past as an actor in B-grade western films
   (C) Reminds Americans of the courage and spirit of early American settlers
   (D) Gives an example that is as old as the divide in political philosophies to which he is speaking
   (E) Appeals to western voters

10. In the closing, the speaker interjects his own story into his speech by:
    (A) Indicating that he has benefitted from opportunities that focused on helping all Americans, regardless of race or religion
    (B) Showing his own pride as Democrat, and pledging to do all he can to defeat Reagan
    (C) Attacking Reagan for the damage that has been done to his family by the President's policies
    (D) Extending an offer to lead bipartisan efforts to solve the problems of the day
    (E) Discussing the varied and diverse racial makeup of the United States.

11. Given the wording of the speech, which of the following is an understanding that the speaker would expect his audience to have in order for its rhetoric to have maximum effect?
    (A) What a "City on a Hill" should really look like
    (B) How Reagan proposed to fix societal problems
    (C) The fact that the speaker's parents were both immigrants from Italy
    (D) The causes of poverty and unemployment in America
    (E) The platform of the Democratic Party

12. The words "wagon train after wagon train" in lines 88–89 primarily serve as a:
    (A) Metaphor to describe the nineteenth-century western settlers
    (B) Simile to describe the people who voted for Roosevelt
    (C) Pun to contrast the two parties together
    (D) Epithet to memorialize Roosevelt
    (E) Parenthesis to emphasize how many people Roosevelt was able to help

13. What can most accurately be said about the words "there are people who sleep in the city streets, in the gutter, where the glitter doesn't show" in lines 26–28?
    (A) They rely on assonance to achieve a rhetorical impact
    (B) They paint an interesting metaphor for the elderly people trembling in basements mentioned earlier
    (C) They show another subterranean group ignored by Reagan
    (D) They create a parallel structure that continues as the speaker identifies other people abandoned by Reagan
    (E) They accuse Reagan of trying to cover up the nation's problems with metaphorical glitter.

14. Which of the following is most true about the phrase "we Democrats believe in something else" that begins the last paragraph (line 83)?
    (A) It was likely an inadvertent pause inserted by the speaker while he sought to articulate his own philosophy
    (B) It creates a mystery that will make the audience pay close attention to the rest of the speech in hopes that it will be solved
    (C) It invites the reader to speculate about how the Democrats would solve the problems facing society
    (D) It was left blank because the speaker wanted to intrigue his audience with a vague statement
    (E) It served to create a small degree of suspense while setting up the next sentence, in order to create repetition and rhetorical intrigue

Questions 15-23. Read the following passage carefully before you select your answers.

(The following excerpt is from a 1747 account of Miss Polly Baker's speech given in front of a Connecticut court.)

May it please the Honourable Bench to indulge me a few Words: I am a poor unhappy Woman; who have no Money to Fee Lawyers to plead for me, being hard put to it to get a tolerable
5 Living. I shall not trouble your Honours with long Speeches; for I have not the presumption to expect, that you may, by any Means, be prevailed on to deviate in your Sentence from the Law, in my Favour. All I humbly hope is, that
10 your Honours would charitably move the Governor's Goodness on my Behalf, that my Fine may be remitted. This is the Fifth Time, Gentlemen, that I have been dragg'd before your Courts on the same Account; twice I have
15 paid heavy Fines, and twice have been brought to public Punishment, for want of Money to pay those Fines. This may have been agreeable to the Laws; I do not dispute it: But since Laws are sometimes unreasonable in themselves,
20 and therefore repealed; and others bear too hard on the Subject in particular Circumstances; and therefore there is left a Power somewhere to dispense with the Execution of them; I take the Liberty to say, that I think this
25 Law, by which I am punished, is both unreasonable in itself, and particularly severe with regard to me, who have always lived an inoffensive Life in the Neighbourhood where I was born, and defy my Enemies (if I have any) to
30 say I ever wrong'd Man, Woman, or Child. Abstracted from the Law, I cannot conceive (may it please your Honours) what the Nature of my Offence is. I have brought Five fine Children into the World, at the Risque of my Life: I
35 have maintained them well by my own Industry, without burthening the Township, and could have done it better, if it had not been for the heavy Charges and Fines I have paid. Can it be a Crime (in the Nature of Things I mean) to

40 add to the Number of the King's Subjects, in a new Country that really wants People? I own I should think it rather a Praise worthy, than a Punishable Action. I have debauch'd no other Woman's Husband, nor inticed any innocent
45 Youth: These Things I never was charged with; nor has any one the least cause of Complaint against me, unless, perhaps the Minister, or the Justice, because I have had Children without being Married, by which they have miss'd a
50 Wedding Fee. But, can even this be a Fault of mine? I appeal to your Honours. You are pleased to allow I don't want Sense; but I must be stupid to the last Degree, not to prefer the honourable State of Wedlock, to the Condition
55 I have lived in. I always was, and still am, willing to enter into it; I doubt not my Behaving well in it, having all the Industry, Frugality, Fertility, and Skill in Economy, appertaining to a good Wife's Character. I defy any Person to
60 say I ever Refused an Offer of that Sort: On the contrary, I readily Consented to the only Proposal of Marriage that ever was made me, which was when I was a Virgin; but too easily confiding in the Person's Sincerity that made
65 it, I unhappily lost my own Honour, by trusting to his; for he got me with Child, and then forsook me: That very Person you all know; he is now become a Magistrate of this County; and I had hopes he would have appeared this
70 Day on the Bench, and have endeavoured to moderate the Court in my Favour; then I should have scorn'd to have mention'd it; but I must Complain of it as unjust and unequal, that my Betrayer and Undoer, the first Cause of
75 all my Faults and Miscarriages (if they must be deemed such) should be advanced to Honour and Power, in the same Government that punishes my Misfortunes with Stripes and Infamy.

I shall be told, 'tis like, that were there no Act of
80 Assembly in the Case, the Precepts of Religion
are violated by my Transgressions. If mine,
then, is a religious Offence, leave it, Gentlemen, to religious Punishments. You have
already excluded me from all the Comforts of
85 your Church Communion: Is not that sufficient? You believe I have offended Heaven, and
must suffer eternal Fire: Will not that be sufficient? What need is there, then, of your additional Fines and Whippings? I own, I do not
90 think as you do; for, if I thought, what you call
a Sin, was really such, I would not presumptu-
ously commit it. But how can it be believed,
that Heaven is angry at my having Children,
when, to the little done by me towards it, God
95 has been pleased to add his divine Skill and
admirable Workmanship in the Formation of
their Bodies, and crown'd it by furnishing
them with rational and immortal Souls? For-
give me Gentlemen, if I talk a little extrava-
100 gantly on these Matters; I am no Divine: But if
you, great Men, (*) must be making Laws, do
not turn natural and useful Actions into
Crimes, by your Prohibitions. Reflect a little on
the horrid Consequences of this Law in partic-
105 ular: What Numbers of procur'd Abortions!
and how many distress'd Mothers have been
driven, by the Terror of Punishment and public Shame, to imbrue, contrary to Nature, their
own trembling Hands in the Blood of their
110 helpless Offspring! Nature would have induc'd
them to nurse it up with a Parent's Fondness.
'Tis the Law therefore, 'tis the Law itself that is
guilty of all these Barbarities and Murders.

Repeal it then, Gentlemen; let it be expung'd
115 for ever from your Books: And on the other
hand, take into your wise Consideration, the
great and growing Number of Batchelors in
the Country, many of whom, from the mean
Fear of the Expence of a Family, have never
120 sincerely and honourably Courted a Woman in
their Lives; and by their Manner of Living,
leave unproduced (which I think is little better
than Murder) Hundreds of their Posterity to
the Thousandth Generation. Is not theirs a
125 greater Offence against the Public Good, than
mine? Compel them then, by a Law, either to
Marry, or pay double the Fine of Fornication
every Year. What must poor young Women do,
whom Custom has forbid to solicit the Men,
130 and who cannot force themselves upon Hus-
bands, when the Laws take no Care to provide
them any, and yet severely punish if they do
their Duty without them? Yes, Gentlemen, I
venture to call it a Duty; 'tis the Duty of the
135 first and great Command of Nature, and of
Nature's God, *Increase and multiply*: A Duty,
from the steady Performance of which nothing
has ever been able to deter me; but for it's Sake,
I have hazarded the Loss of the public Esteem,
140 and frequently incurr'd public Disgrace and
Punishment; and therefore ought, in my humble Opinion, instead of a Whipping, to have a
Statue erected to my Memory.

(*) *Turning to some Gentlemen of the Assembly,
then in Court.*

The Maryland Gazette, August 11, 1747; first
printed April 15, 1747

15. When read in context of the entire
document, the phrase "honourable" in the
first line can best be described as:
(A) Deferential
(B) Ironic
(C) Sarcastic
(D) Diffident
(E) Lamenting

16. The anaphora in lines 14–15 is meant to
relate a sense of:
(A) Burden
(B) Anger
(C) Ersatz
(D) Conviction
(E) Humor

17. What is the chief purpose of the section ranging from lines 31–50?
    (A) To question the convictions of the judges
    (B) To introduce a paradox
    (C) To refute a legal code on religious terms
    (D) To mock the local religion
    (E) To provide a logical refutation of a legal code

18. Baker's discussion of the loss of her "honour" on and around line 65 invites what comparison?
    (A) The difference in opportunities for men and women in the society
    (B) The differences between an honor and a merit based society
    (C) The differences between a judge and a preacher
    (D) The differences in lifestyles of men and woman in the society
    (E) The differences between publicly bestowed titles of honor and the personal sense of honor lost when wronged

19. When discussing the punishments she has already received from the church, Baker is most likely attempting to:
    (A) Seem suppliant to the community and ask for forgiveness
    (B) Evoke a religious defense of her actions based on biblical passages that would support her behavior
    (C) Seek asylum from the law as an agent of the church
    (D) Force the judge's ire unto the local church elders
    (E) Evoke a sense of "double jeopardy," and argue that she should not be punished for the same offense twice

20. Near the end of her speech, Baker asks the court to consider the conduct of the many bachelors in the county (line 117). She likely included this in order to:
    (A) Show that others are in a similar plight to her own, but go unpunished
    (B) Demonstrate compassion for those trying her
    (C) Question whether family is important anyway
    (D) Indict the men of the area for refusing to wed the single women
    (E) Lament the high divorce rate in the area

21. The introduction of the God of Nature in the closing lines serves what chief purpose?
    (A) It offers a conciliatory tone by providing a deity shared by all.
    (B) It provides a sharp contrast to the Christian doctrines upon which the laws of her society are built.
    (C) It antagonizes the justices by questioning their belief system.
    (D) It advocates that she be allowed to live more freely outside the community.
    (E) It adds to her sense of logos by claiming divine aid.

22. Which of the following are present in this speech?
        I. Irony
        II. Satire
        III. Deference

    (A) I only
    (B) II only
    (C) III only
    (D) I and II only
    (E) All of the above

23. After reading Polly Baker's entire speech, which of the following is the most likely explanation for why one of the town justices chose to marry her the next day?
    (A) He hoped to quiet her protests by using a husband's authority to silence his wife.
    (B) He thought he could orchestrate a scheme upon marrying her that would force her to move out of the state.
    (C) He believed he could teach her Christian virtue and save her soul.
    (D) He had fathered her children, and was ashamed upon being "outed" in her speech.
    (E) He hoped that he would inherit her considerable wealth upon marriage.

24. Which of the following best explains what Baker means in line 129 when she writes "whom custom has forbid to solicit the men"?
    (A) Women cannot apply for employment from men, giving them unequal economic opportunity.
    (B) In the society, prostitution is illegal for women, but is not illegal for men.
    (C) Women are forbidden from doing business with men, limiting their ability to turn a profit.
    (D) Women are unable, according to tradition, to propose marriage to a man.
    (E) In the society, it is illegal for a woman to initiate a sexual relationship with a man.

(The following passage is from a 1916 study composed by a leading reformer and progressive.)

It is most fortunate, therefore, that in some subtle fashion these old people, reviewing the long road they have travelled, are able to transmute their own untoward experiences into
5 that which seems to make even the most wretched life acceptable. This may possibly be due to an instinct of self-preservation, which checks the devastating bitterness that would result did they recall over and over again the
10 sordid detail of events long past; it is even possible that those people who were not able thus to inhibit their bitterness have died earlier, for as one old man recently reminded me, "It is a true word that worry can kill a cat."

15 This permanent and elemental function of Memory was graphically demonstrated at Hull-House during a period of several weeks when we were reported to be harboring within its walls a so-called "Devil Baby."

20 The knowledge of his existence burst upon the residents of Hull-House one day when three Italian women, with an excited rush through the door, demanded that he be shown to them. No amount of denial convinced them that he
25 was not there, for they knew exactly what he was like with his cloven hoofs, his pointed ears and diminutive tail; the Devil Baby had, moreover, been able to speak as soon as he was born and was most shockingly profane.

30 The three women were but the forerunners of a veritable multitude; for six weeks from every part of the city and suburbs the streams of visitors to this mythical baby poured in all day long and so far into the night that the regular activi-
35 ties of the settlement were almost swamped.

The Italian version, with a hundred variations, dealt with a pious Italian girl married to an atheist. Her husband in a rage had torn a holy picture from the bedroom wall saying that he
40 would quite as soon have a devil in the house as such a thing, whereupon the devil incarnated himself in her coming child. As soon as the Devil Baby was born, he ran about the table shaking his finger in deep reproach at his
45 father, who finally caught him and, in fear and trembling, brought him to Hull-House.

When the residents there, in spite of the baby's shocking appearance, wishing to save his soul, took him to church for baptism, they found
50 that the shawl was empty and the Devil Baby, fleeing from the holy water, was running lightly over the backs of the pews.

The Jewish version, again with variations, was to the effect that the father of six daughters had
55 said before the birth of a seventh child that he would rather have a devil in the family than another girl, whereupon the Devil Baby promptly appeared.

Save for a red automobile which occasionally
60 figured in the story and a stray cigar which, in some versions, the new-born child had snatched from his father's lips, the tale might have been fashioned a thousand years ago.

Although the visitors to the Devil Baby included
65 persons of every degree of prosperity and education, even physicians and trained nurses, who assured us of their scientific interest, the story constantly demonstrated the power of an old wives' tale among thousands of men and women

70 in modern society who are living in a corner of their own, their vision fixed, their intelligence held by some iron chain of silent habit.

To such primitive people the metaphor apparently is still the very "stuff of life," or rather no
75 other form of statement reaches them; the tremendous tonnage of current writing for them has no existence. It was in keeping with their simple habits that the reputed presence of the Devil Baby should not reach the newspapers
80 until the fifth week of his sojourn at Hull-House after thousands of people had already been informed of his whereabouts by the old method of passing news from mouth to mouth . . .

During the weeks of excitement it was the old
85 women who really seemed to have come into their own, and perhaps the most significant result of the incident was the reaction of the

story upon them. It stirred their minds and memories as with a magic touch, it loosened
90 their tongues and revealed the inner life and thoughts of those who are so often inarticulate. They are accustomed to sit at home and to hear the younger members of the family speak of affairs quite outside their own experiences,
95 sometimes in a language they do not understand, and at best in quick glancing phrases which they cannot follow; "More than half the time I can't tell what they are talking about," is an oft-repeated complaint. The story of the
100 Devil Baby evidently put into their hands the sort of material with which they were accustomed to deal. They had long used such tales in their unremitting efforts at family discipline, ever since they had frightened their first chil-
105 dren into awed silence by tales of bugaboo men who prowled in the darkness.

25. In line 6, the pronoun "this" most likely refers to:
(A) The subtleties employed by the elderly in their daily conduct
(B) The ability to transmute unhappy incidents into acceptable memories
(C) The wretched lives most elderly people were experiencing in 1916
(D) The "long road" an elderly person has travelled
(E) The lucky circumstances to have reached old age while living in a slum

26. The quotation at the end of the first paragraph serves which of the following purposes?
    I. It reaffirms the author's musing by introducing a supporting idiom
    II. It introduces a corroborating study that supports her conclusion
    III. It provides a glimpse into the thoughts of the elderly about whom she is writing

(A) I only
(B) II only
(C) I, II, and II
(D) I and II only
(E) I and III only

27. How does the speaker choose to speak of the Devil-Baby throughout her reflection, starting with its introduction in line 19?
    (A) In a sarcastic manner, excoriating those foolish enough to believe in one
    (B) In a lighthearted fashion, laughing at the customs of immigrants
    (C) With intrigue, questioning how the realm of the supernatural conflicts with our own
    (D) In a deadpan tone, inviting the reader to examine the ideas themselves
    (E) With embarrassment, that such beliefs should continue in the twentieth century

28. The semicolon and subsequent clauses in lines 27–29 chiefly serve to:
    (A) Demonstrate the extent of the women's beliefs by recounting even more of the corroborating details they supplied
    (B) Provide contrary evidence to question the veracity of the women's claims
    (C) Question the superstition behind all claims of demonic forces
    (D) Reflect on the absolute certainty with which the women held their convictions
    (E) Ridicule the women for providing such a stock description of the alleged imp

29. Which of the following metaphoric phrases is most similar to that employed in lines 30–31?
    (A) The calm before the storm
    (B) The first fallen leaves of autumn
    (C) The first shots of a battle
    (D) Separating the wheat from the chaff
    (E) Putting the shoe on the other foot

30. In the context of the passage, "the residents there" mentioned in line 47 refers to
    (A) The parents of the Devil Baby
    (B) The speaker and her associates
    (C) The three Italian women
    (D) The local priests
    (E) The city's social workers

31. What is the most striking similarity between the Italian and Jewish "versions" of the Devil-Baby story, as related by the speaker?
    (A) They both center around an egregious sin committed by the fathers.
    (B) The Devil Baby is an act of punishment bestowed by god upon the offending families.
    (C) The mothers do not stand up enough against their husband's abuses.
    (D) They both include a red automobile.
    (E) Both stories cite an imprudent evocation of the devil by a rash father as the source of their conflicts.

32. The discussion of the doctors and nurses who came in search of the Devil Baby in line 66 serves primarily to:
    (A) Question the credibility of the medical profession and call for more scientific training
    (B) Demonstrate the broad appeal that the story had across many different strata and spectrums of society
    (C) Show how easily humans can be duped
    (D) Highlight the attempts made by the scientific classes to disprove the Devil Baby's existence
    (E) Reflect on the carnival-like atmosphere of the daily gatherings of crowds outside Hull House

33. In context of the entire passage, the section from lines 64–72 might best be seen as:
    (A) An extension of the driving anecdote beyond the slums and into the professional classes
    (B) An aside about the power of "old wives tales" to shape society
    (C) A transition from an extended anecdote into a scholarly discussion
    (D) A defense of modern society against attacks from traditionalists
    (E) An inquiry into the roots and causes of folk-lore

34. What of the following is the best definition of what the speaker means when she writes that the metaphor is "the very stuff of life" in line 74?
    (A) That despite massive scientific writings to the contrary, the immigrants refuse to believe modern conceptions of the world
    (B) That metaphors persist as a form of communication and value-sharing despite advances in other realms of education and science
    (C) That without superstition, immigrant cultures would wither away
    (D) That metaphors should be included in any attempt to communicate with inner city dwellers
    (E) That all humans are drawn to metaphors as a way to consume and process the happenings of the world

35. Which of the following criticisms could best be leveled at the speaker's passage by a modern day reader?
    (A) It lacks proper introspection, and should consider the reason for metaphor in immigrant communities.
    (B) It lacks a deep enough investigation and reporting into the details of the Devil Baby rumor.
    (C) It is highly elitist, and therefore writes with a debilitating bias against its subjects.
    (D) It is too sympathetic to its subjects, and would benefit from a more detached lens.
    (E) It lacks the level of inquiry requisite for a sophisticated study and considers a topic about which the author has no expertise.

36. Which of the following is not a possible cause discussed by the speaker for the appeal of the Devil Baby rumor to older members of the inner city community?
    (A) It gave them an opportunity to use a fantastic story to encourage discipline.
    (B) It used a supernatural idea they could relate to.
    (C) It reverted back to traditional cultures, unlike the current trends spoken of by their children and grandchildren.
    (D) It jolted them with concrete evidence of a phenomenon they had always suspected but could never prove.
    (E) It allowed them to ignore their tired and saddened states by participating in community gossip.

37. To the extent that the word "newspapers" is used in line 79 to indicate the attitudes of the secular, logical, fact-based world, the term is used as a:
    (A) Simile
    (B) Anachronism
    (C) Anaphora
    (D) Parenthetical
    (E) Metonymy

38. After reading the entire passage, which of the following documents might have the closest resemblance, in method and style, to this one?
    (A) A pious priest examining a satanic cult
    (B) A biologist examining variances in a specific species
    (C) A detective writing a report of his investigation
    (D) An anthropologist examining popular stories in a voodoo culture
    (E) A doctor outlining a method of treatment for a specific disease

39. In context of the entire passage, the first paragraph primarily serves what purpose?
    (A) It is an indictment of the lifestyle of an entire class of Americans.
    (B) It is a memoir about a specific time in the speaker's life.
    (C) It is an introduction to a feminist manifesto.
    (D) It is a brief musing on the eventual subject of her essay.
    (E) It sets up a parallel structure that will guide the rest of the passage.

40. In the context of the paragraph, the phrase "fleeing from the holy water" in line 51 is intended to be read
    (A) Metaphorically
    (B) Skepticly
    (C) Literally
    (D) Mockingly
    (E) Abashedly

41. Which of the following is the best simile for the description the speaker provides of the superstitious men and women in lines 69–72?
    (A) Prisoners trying to throw off their chains because they're unjustly shackled
    (B) Students trying to learn a new language through an immersion process
    (C) People in a cave turned away from the light and watching the shadows on the wall instead
    (D) Sons rebelling against the traditions of their families and communities
    (E) A long line of lemmings following one anther as they jump off a cliff

Questions 42-53. Read the following passage carefully before you select your answers.

(This passage is excerpted from an 1833 message to Congress by the President of the United States, Andrew Jackson.)

The present policy of the Government is but a continuation of the same progressive change by a milder process. The tribes which occupied the countries now constituting the Eastern
5 States were annihilated or have melted away to make room for the whites. The waves of population and civilization are rolling to the westward, and we now propose to acquire the countries occupied by the red men of the
10 South and West by a fair exchange, and, at the expense of the United States, to send them to a land where their existence may be prolonged and perhaps made perpetual.

Doubtless it will be painful to leave the graves
15 of their fathers; but what do they more than our ancestors did or than our children are now doing? To better their condition in an unknown land our forefathers left all that was dear in earthly objects. Our children by thou-
20 sands yearly leave the land of their birth to seek new homes in distant regions. Does Humanity weep at these painful separations from everything, animate and inanimate, with which the young heart has become entwined? Far from it.
25 It is rather a source of joy that our country affords scope where our young population may range unconstrained in body or in mind, developing the power and faculties of man in their highest perfection. These remove hun-
30 dreds and almost thousands of miles at their own expense, purchase the lands they occupy, and support themselves at their new homes from the moment of their arrival. Can it be cruel in this Government when, by events
35 which it can not control, the Indian is made discontented in his ancient home to purchase his lands, to give him a new and extensive territory, to pay the expense of his removal, and support him a year in his new abode? How
40 many thousands of our own people would

gladly embrace the opportunity of removing to the West on such conditions! If the offers made to the Indians were extended to them, they would be hailed with gratitude and joy.

45 And is it supposed that the wandering savage has a stronger attachment to his home than the settled, civilized Christian? Is it more afflicting to him to leave the graves of his fathers than it is to our brothers and children? Rightly consid-
50 ered, the policy of the General Government toward the red man is not only liberal, but generous. He is unwilling to submit to the laws of the States and mingle with their population. To save him from this alternative, or perhaps utter
55 annihilation, the General Government kindly offers him a new home, and proposes to pay the whole expense of his removal and settlement.

In the consummation of a policy originating at an early period, and steadily pursued by every
60 administration within the present century—so just to the states and so generous to the Indians—the executive feels it has a right to expect the cooperation of Congress and of all good and disinterested men. The states, moreover,
65 have a right to demand it. It was substantially a part of the compact which made them members of our Confederacy. With Georgia there is an express contract; with the new states an implied one of equal obligation. Why, in
70 authorizing Ohio, Indiana, Illinois, Missouri, Mississippi, and Alabama to form constitutions and become separate states, did Congress include within their limits extensive tracts of Indian lands, and, in some instances, powerful
75 Indian tribes? Was it not understood by both parties that the power of the states was to be coextensive with their limits, and that, with all convenient dispatch, the general government should extinguish the Indian title and remove

every obstruction to the complete jurisdiction
of the state governments over the soil? Probably not one of those states would have accepted
a separate existence—certainly it would never
have been granted by Congress—had it been
understood that they were to be confined forever to those small portions of their nominal
territory the Indian title to which had at the
time been extinguished.

It is, therefore, a duty which this government
owes to the new states to extinguish as soon as
possible the Indian title to all lands which
Congress themselves nave included within
their limits. When this is done the duties of the
general government in relation to the states
and the Indians within their limits are at an
end. The Indians may leave the state or not, as
they choose. The purchase of their lands does
not alter in the least their personal relations
with the state government. No act of the general government has ever been deemed necessary to give the states jurisdiction over the
persons of the Indians. That they possess by
virtue of their sovereign power within their
own limits in as full a manner before as after
the purchase of the Indian lands; nor can this
government add to or diminish it.

May we not hope, therefore, that all good citizens, and none more zealously than those who
think the Indians oppressed by subjection to
the laws of the States, will unite in attempting
to open the eyes of those children of the forest
to their true condition, and by a speedy
removal to relieve them from all the evils, real
or imaginary, present or prospective, with
which they may be supposed to be threatened.

42. The phrase "The waves of population and
civilization are rolling to the westward" in
lines 6–7 is an example of:
(A) Assonance
(B) Personification
(C) Metaphor
(D) Anthropomorphism
(E) Satire

43. Given the tone of the document, the phrase
"fair exchange" in the first paragraph (line
10) is meant to be a contrast to:
(A) Unscrupulous trading practices of the
past, in which Indians deceived whites
by trading poor quality goods with them
(B) The deceitful and violent practices
visited by many early settlers on Indians
(C) The lack of a regulated system to guide
the trading economy between the whites
and Indians
(D) A cultural war that had prohibited
whites and Indians from appreciating
each others values
(E) The earlier lack of a standard unit of
currency by which to do business

44. The phrase "prolonged and perhaps made
perpetual" (lines 12–13) draws most of its
rhetorical appeal from its
(A) Ethos
(B) Logos
(C) Mythos
(D) Assonance
(E) Optimism

45. In the second and third paragraphs, Jackson
uses a series of rhetorical questions in order
to:
(A) Incite sympathy for the situation of the
natives
(B) Condemn the Indians for their
godlessness
(C) Draw a parallel to contrast the attitudes
between the Indians and the whites
(D) Invoke the Socratic method to prove his
point
(E) Solicit information from his audience
on the nature of Indian attitudes

46. Which of the following facts, if proven true, would best counter Jackson's argument in lines 45–49?
    (A) That Indians were warlike only because they feared whites would encroach upon their land otherwise
    (B) That Indians held a deep-seated distrust of Christianity and other monotheistic religions
    (C) That Indian religions tended to be heavily grounded in a particular area, holding specific mountaintops, lakes, and streams as holy ground.
    (D) That Indian religions forbade communications with white men
    (E) That Christian missionaries had tried to convert natives, with little success

47. The relationship Jackson describes between "General Government" and the "red man" in lines 50–57 can best be seen as;
    (A) Condescending
    (B) Paternalistic
    (C) Accomodating
    (D) Confrontational
    (E) Affectionate

48. Jackson's third-person reference to himself in line 62 provides a sense of
    (A) Humility
    (B) Detachment
    (C) Gravitas
    (D) Antagonism
    (E) Futility

49. Which of the following best paraphrases Jackson's argument from lines 69–88?
    (A) In drawing state borders, Congress would not have included land within each new state unless Congress wanted it to be settled by whites.
    (B) In drawing state borders, Congress wanted to make sure that some of the land of each state was kept as reservation for the Natives living there .
    (C) New states like Illinois, Ohio, Indiana, Alabama, and Mississippi should not provoke the native inhabitants, and accede to the Indians' demands for land and independence.
    (D) Now that Congress has made all these new states, they shouldn't make any more states, keeping the rest of the land for native use.
    (E) There were so few Indians living in the new states when they entered the union that the government need not worry about their fate.

50. The reflection on "jurisdiction" (line 80) articulates what idea?
    (A) That states should convene courts to hear land disputes between Indians and whites
    (B) That the national government should create a Bureau of Indian Affairs to settle disputes that might arise
    (C) That Indians should be consulted in deciding what policies each state will pursue
    (D) That states already have full legal power to govern the natives in their state, making government intervention questionable from the outset
    (E) That the individual states would need to prove that they should be put in control of negotiations with Indians

51. Jackson's final paragraph of this document could best be described as a:
    (A) Rebuke of his opponents
    (B) Call for united action
    (C) Mockery of the Indians
    (D) Challenge to the Indians
    (E) Condemnation of injustices

52. After reading the entire passage, which of the following best characterizes Jackson's attitude towards the annihilation and melting away that was the fate of Indians on the east coast?
    (A) He sees it as a tragedy that must not be allowed to happen again.
    (B) He sees it as a convincing argument to allow the Indians to keep their gains.
    (C) He sees it as an outcome to attempt to avoid, but to recourse to if necessary.
    (D) He thinks that the problems of the past will be forgotten if a more progressive policy is introduced.
    (E) He thinks that Christians should not engage in such destructive behavior.

53. Which of the following phrases is the best example of a euphemism?
    (A) "Express contract" (line 68)
    (B) "Good citizens" (lines 112–113)
    (C) "Milder process" (line 3)
    (D) "Made discontented" (lines 35–36)
    (E) "Present century" (line 60)

Question 1: Synthesis

The Electoral College has come under increased scrutiny over the last decade, and historians have pointed out that there are four elections in American History where the person receiving the most popular votes did not become president. Many charge that the Electoral College is undemocratic and should be abolished. Proponents of the process, however, point out that the Electoral College ensures that states have a better say in the election, and that it guards against the tyranny of the majority.

Read the following sources carefully. Then, in an essay that synthesizes at least three sources for support, take a position that defends, qualifies, or challenges the claim that the Electoral College is undemocratic and should be abolished.

Make sure your argument is central to the essay. Be sure to use the sources provided to help elucidate and support your position. While it is not necessary that you use the MLA or APA format in citing your sources, you should clearly identify those sources that you use to help develop and support your opinion. You may identify these sources by referring to them as Source A, B, C, etc., or you may provide identifying information in parenthesis.

Source A: "The Constitution of the United States"
Source B: "How the Electoral College Works"
Source C: "U.S. Department of State Outline of U.S. History"
Source D: United States National Archives and Records Administration
Source E: Hamilton
Source F: "United States Presidential Election, 2000"
Source G: "United States Presidential Election of 1860"

The following is from the Constitution of the United States of America.

The executive Power shall be vested in a President of the United States of America. He shall hold his Office during the Term of four Years, and, together with the Vice President, chosen for the same Term, be elected, as follows . . .

Each State shall appoint, in such Manner as the Legislature thereof may direct, a Number of Electors, equal to the whole Number of Senators and Representatives to which the State may be entitled in the Congress: but no Senator or Representative, or Person holding an Office of Trust or Profit under the United States, shall be appointed an Elector . . .

The Electors shall meet in their respective states and vote by ballot for President and Vice-President, one of whom, at least, shall not be an inhabitant of the same state with themselves; they shall name in their ballots the person voted for as President, and in distinct ballots the person voted for as Vice-President…and transmit sealed to the seat of the government of the United States…and if no person have [a majority of the votes], then from the persons having the highest numbers not exceeding three on the list of those voted for as President, the House of Representatives shall choose immediately, by ballot, the President.

The following is information regarding the Electoral College provided by a governmental website.

On the Tuesday following the first Monday of November in years divisible by four, the people in each State cast their ballots for the party slate of Electors representing their choice for president and vice president (although as a matter of practice, general election ballots normally say "Electors for" each set of candidates rather than list the individual Electors on each slate).

Whichever party slate wins the most popular votes in the State becomes that State's Electors—so that, in effect, whichever presidential ticket gets the most popular votes in a State wins all the Electors of that State. [The two exceptions to this are Maine and Nebraska where two Electors are chosen by statewide popular vote and the remainder by the popular vote within each Congressional district].

On the Monday following the second Wednesday of December (as established in Federal law) each State's Electors meet in their respective State capitals and cast their electoral votes—one for president and one for vice president.

In order to prevent Electors from voting only for "favorite sons" of their home State, at least one of their votes must be for a person from outside their State (though this is seldom a problem since the parties have consistently nominated presidential and vice presidential candidates from different States).

The electoral votes are then sealed and transmitted from each State to the President of the Senate who, on the following January 6, opens and reads them before both houses of the Congress.

The following is an outline of United States history provided by the United States State Department.

Personality and sectional allegiance played important roles in determining the outcome of the election [of 1824]. [John Quincy] Adams won the electoral votes from New England and most of New York; [Henry] Clay won Kentucky, Ohio, and Missouri; [Andrew] Jackson won the Southeast, Illinois, Indiana, the Carolinas, Pennsylvania, Maryland, and New Jersey; and [William] Crawford won Virginia, Georgia, and Delaware. No candidate gained a majority in the Electoral College, so, according to the provisions of the Constitution, the election was thrown into the House of Representatives, where Clay was the most influential figure. He supported Adams, who gained the presidency . . .

Though he governed honestly and efficiently, Adams was not a popular president. He failed in his effort to institute a national system of roads and canals. His coldly intellectual temperament did not win friends. Jackson, by contrast, had enormous popular appeal and a strong political organization . . . mounting a strong anti-Adams campaign, they accused the president of a "corrupt bargain" for naming Clay secretary of state. In the election of 1828, Jackson defeated Adams by an overwhelming electoral majority.

The following information was originally composed by the U.S. Federal Election Commission and then made available through government archives.

Reference sources indicate that over the past 200 years, over 700 proposals have been introduced in Congress to reform or eliminate the Electoral College. There have been more proposals for Constitutional amendments on changing the Electoral College than on any other subject. The American Bar Association has criticized the Electoral College as "archaic" and "ambiguous" and its polling showed 69 percent of lawyers favored abolishing it in 1987. But surveys of political scientists have supported continuation of the Electoral College. Public opinion polls have shown Americans favored abolishing it by majorities of 58 percent in 1967; 81 percent in 1968; and 75 percent in 1981.

Opinions on the viability of the Electoral College system may be affected by attitudes toward third parties. Third parties have not fared well in the Electoral College system. Candidates with regional appeal such as Governor Thurmond in 1948 and Governor Wallace in 1968, won blocs of electoral votes in the South. Neither come close to seriously challenging the major party winner, but they may have affected the overall outcome of the election.

The following excerpt is from Alexander Hamilton's Federalist No. 68.

The [electoral college] process of election affords a moral certainty, that the office of President will never fall to the lot of any man who is not in an eminent degree endowed with the requisite qualifications. Talents for low intrigue, and the little arts of popularity, may alone suffice to elevate a man to the first honors in a single State; but it will require other talents, and a different kind of merit, to establish him in the esteem and confidence of the whole Union, or of so considerable a portion of it as would be necessary to make him a successful candidate for the distinguished office of President of the United States. It will not be too strong to say, that there will be a constant probability of seeing the station filled by characters pre-eminent for ability and virtue.

"Presidential Election, 2000." National Atlas home page. N.p., n.d. Web. 4 Jan. 2013. <http://nationalatlas.gov/printable/printableViewer.htm?imgF=images/preview/elections/08_elect13.gif&imgW=764&imgH=585>.

The following chart was created by the National Atlas of the United States.

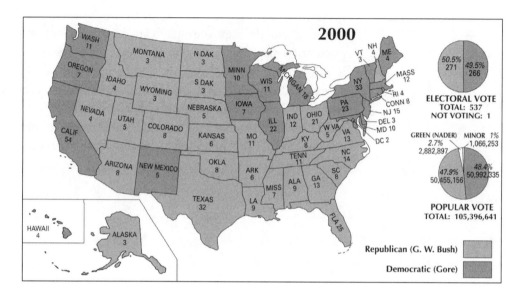

The following chart was created by the National Atlas of the United States.

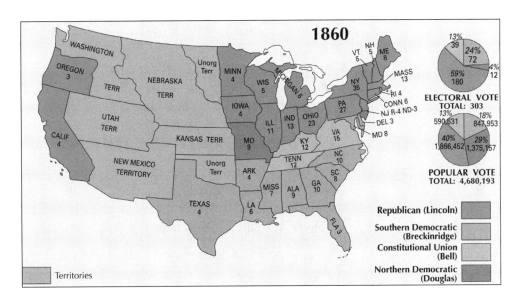

Question 2: Analysis

(Suggested time: 40 minutes. This question counts
for one-third of the total essay section score.)

The speech below was given by President George W. Bush on the evening of September 11, 2001. In the speech, President Bush addresses the American people in response to the terrorist attacks on American soil. Read the speech carefully and consider its purpose. Then write an essay in which you analyze the strategies President Bush uses in achieving this purpose.

Good evening. Today, our fellow citizens, our way of life, our very freedom came under attack in a series of deliberate and deadly terrorist acts. The victims were in airplanes, or in their offices; secretaries, businessmen and women, military and federal workers; moms and dads, friends and neighbors. Thou-
5   sands of lives were suddenly ended by evil, despicable acts of terror.

The pictures of airplanes flying into buildings, fires burning, huge structures collapsing, have filled us with disbelief, terrible sadness, and a quiet, unyielding anger. These acts of mass murder were intended to frighten our nation into chaos and retreat. But they have failed; our country is strong.

10   A great people has been moved to defend a great nation. Terrorist attacks can shake the foundations of our biggest buildings, but they cannot touch the foundation of America. These acts shattered steel, but they cannot dent the steel of American resolve.

America was targeted for attack because we're the brightest beacon for freedom
15   and opportunity in the world. And no one will keep that light from shining.

Today, our nation saw evil, the very worst of human nature. And we responded with the best of America—with the daring of our rescue workers, with the caring for strangers and neighbors who came to give blood and help in any way they could.

20   Immediately following the first attack, I implemented our government's emergency response plans. Our military is powerful, and it's prepared. Our emergency teams are working in New York City and Washington, D.C. to help with local rescue efforts.

Our first priority is to get help to those who have been injured, and to take
25   every precaution to protect our citizens at home and around the world from further attacks.

The functions of our government continue without interruption. Federal agencies in Washington which had to be evacuated today are reopening for essential personnel tonight, and will be open for business tomorrow. Our
30   financial institutions remain strong, and the American economy will be open for business, as well.

The search is underway for those who are behind these evil acts. I've directed the full resources of our intelligence and law enforcement communities to find those responsible and to bring them to justice. We will make no distinction between the terrorists who committed these acts and those who harbor them.

I appreciate so very much the members of Congress who have joined me in strongly condemning these attacks. And on behalf of the American people, I thank the many world leaders who have called to offer their condolences and assistance.

America and our friends and allies join with all those who want peace and security in the world, and we stand together to win the war against terrorism. Tonight, I ask for your prayers for all those who grieve, for the children whose worlds have been shattered, for all whose sense of safety and security has been threatened. And I pray they will be comforted by a power greater than any of us, spoken through the ages in Psalm 23: "Even though I walk through the valley of the shadow of death, I fear no evil, for You are with me."

This is a day when all Americans from every walk of life unite in our resolve for justice and peace. America has stood down enemies before, and we will do so this time. None of us will ever forget this day. Yet, we go forward to defend freedom and all that is good and just in our world.

Thank you. Good night, and God bless America.

Question 3: Argument

(Suggested time: 40 minutes. This question counts
for one-third of the total essay section score.)

Character cannot be developed in ease and quiet. Only through experience of trial and suffering can the soul be strengthened, vision cleared, ambition inspired, and success achieved.

—Helen Keller

Consider this quotation about character from the American author and political activist, Helen Keller. Then write an essay that defends, challenges, or qualifies Keller's assertion about role of trial and suffering in the development of one's character. Be sure to support your assertions with evidence drawn from your studies, your personal experience, or your observations of the world at large.

Answers and Explanations for Sample Exams

AP® Literature Sample Practice Exam A

from New York Governor Mario Cuomo's 1984 keynote address at the Democratic Convention

ANSWERS AND EXPLANATIONS

Multiple-Choice Questions

1. **(D) is correct.** The main purpose of this speech is to attack Reagan for expressing what appears to be an increasingly uninformed and shallow view of American society.

2. **(B) is correct.** Cuomo spends substantial time articulating what a real American "City upon a Hill" might look like.

3. **(D) is correct.** In both of these instances, a particular location is used to indicate a broader way of living and thinking about society.

4. **(B) is correct.** By expanding the City upon a Hill metaphor to be inclusive of all society, Cuomo is showing where Reagan's comments fell short.

5. **(E) is correct.** The contempt is clear in the passage, as Cuomo criticizes Reagan for his lack of perception of the true conditions in America.

6. **(C) is correct.** In each of these paragraphs, Cuomo speaks as though Reagan were on the stage with him.

7. **(B) is correct.** While one might look deeper into the themes of Dickens's text, the role of the line in the speech is one of rhetorical frivolity to entertain/engage the listener or reader.

8. **(C) is correct.** The "maybe if you" repetition counts for Anaphora, and the Appalachia/Lackawanna references are good examples of a Metonymic structure in that specific places represent broader parts of the population.

9. **(D) is correct.** Cuomo introduces the wagon train directly after discussing the historical divide between the two parties; moreover, none of the other options is a logical choice.

10. **(A) is correct.** Hence the "some of us in this room are only here" reference.

- **11. (A) is correct.** Cuomo expects that his audience will have at least some idea of Winthrop's document in order for them to understand the contrast between that utopia and the current state of society.
- **12. (E) is correct.** The words are a parenthesis as they interrupt the typical flow of the sentence, and they emphasize the many recipients of New Deal aid.
- **13. (A) is correct.** "Glitter/Gutter" are phonetically similar, and their proximity produces an intriguing impact on both reader and listener alike. The other answers all contain factual or logical flaws.
- **14. (E) is correct.** The first sentence sets up a repetitive anaphora with the second, and also provides a small degree of intrigue.

Miss Polly Baker's speech, recorded in 1747 by Ben Franklin

ANSWERS AND EXPLANATIONS

Multiple-Choice Questions

▌ **15. (B) is correct.** A major theme of this speech is questioning what constitutes honorable behavior, ultimately finding that those who would punish Polly for her actions have none of it.

▌ **16. (A) is correct.** Given the argumentative nature of her speech, the anaphora is intended to show the burdens she has already had to overcome.

▌ **17. (E) is correct.** While agreeing that the law is clearly against her, Baker uses this section in an attempt to demonstrate that she has committed no crime if her conduct is viewed logically.

▌ **18. (E) is correct.** A large theme of this work is the meaning of honor, and what actions are truly honorable. She makes this clear when she contrasts the lost honor of being tricked into losing her virginity with the false honor bestowed upon the justices.

▌ **19. (E) is correct.** Though written before the U.S. Constitution, the sense of single punishments for single offenses is clearly the chief motivation for her to evoke the Church's prior actions towards her.

▌ **20. (D) is correct.** Once again, Baker is attempting to question the logic of the proceedings by wondering how the women are supposed to live in wedlock if men refuse to marry them.

▌ **21. (B) is correct.** The true crime in this case is that the society continues to uphold laws contrary to the natural logic of humanity.

▌ **22. (A) is correct.** Baker often comments on the ironic situation of being charged with a crime for raising children as best she can, while their father is honored for neglecting them. She is never deferential, and avoids satire.

▌ **23. (D) is correct.** While some of the other answers are logically possible, Baker explicitly mentions that one of the judges in town has fathered her children, and Franklin's inclusion of the detail about the next day's marriage makes it the most likely conclusion.

▌ **24. (D) is correct.** Baker writes this in the context of reflecting on her difficulty in finding a husband; moreover, the word "custom" implies that it is not technically illegal, but rather taboo to do so.

from Jane Addams from her 1916 study "The Long Road of Woman's Memory"

ANSWERS AND EXPLANATIONS

Multiple-Choice Questions

▌ **25. (B) is correct.** Though the other answers all describe key words in the first paragraph, "this" refers to the main process of the first sentence: the way humans are able to create memories.

▌ **26. (E) is correct.** There is nothing scientific or factual to support the old man's saying (II); instead, it is an idiom that agrees with Addams's idea (I) that is generated by a representative of the group she is considering (III).

▌ **27. (D) is correct.** While the topic seems foolish to the modern reader, Addams never comments on it in anything other than a frank manner, studying the rumor from a sociological sense rather than mocking it as a critic.

▌ **28. (A) is correct.** Extending the sentence gives an even greater sense of just how fervently they had believed the story and the extent to which they invented evidence to support it.

▌ **29. (B) is correct.** The few (forerunners) herald the many (multitude) just as the first falling leaves of Autumn indicate the many more to come.

▌ **30. (B) is correct.** By using the third-person, Addams recounts the role that she and her associates are claimed to have played in the story.

▌ **31. (E) is correct.** In both stories, it is an ill-conceived choice of words which invites the scourge upon the parents.

▌ **32. (B) is correct.** Though Addams may have other axes to grind with the medical staff, the main purpose of this detail is to show that the tale appealed to a broad swath of society.

▌ **33. (C) is correct.** In this paragraph, Addams leaves the story of the events surrounding the Devil Baby behind and moves into a discussion of why the tale had such appeal within the community.

▌ **34. (B) is correct.** Addams does not necessarily claim that the people who came to Hull House because of the rumor were rebuking science; instead, she claims that humans seem to supplement current events with folk traditions and metaphorical stories.

▌ **35. (C) is correct.** Calling the visitors primitive and simple, it is fairly evident that Addams believes them to be from a different stratum of society.

▌ **36. (D) is correct.** There is no concrete evidence ever given, and indeed the whole passage is written with the understanding that no Devil Baby existed.

▌ **37. (E) is correct.** Metonymy uses a particular attribute to describe an entire body; in this case, the newspaper represents the kind of people who read it and value logic and facts.

▌ **38. (D) is correct.** Addams approaches her subjects as beings of a separate culture, whose beliefs should be studied in order to gain a better understanding, the same way an anthropologist might encounter the practices of a different culture.

39. (D) is correct. The first paragraph takes up the issues of memory and metaphor which are discussed in greater detail after the anecdote is told.

40. (C) is correct. The paragraph, which accounts the Italian women's version of events, discusses the Devil Baby as they believe he exists and acts. Thus, the running from the holy water is an actual act that happened, according to the women whose perspective dictates the passage.

41. (C) is correct. Addams views these people as metaphorically shackled to tradition, but voluntarily looking into the corner, just as these people look at the shadows on the wall rather than turning around and seeing the source.

Excerpt from an 1833 message to congress by Andrew Jackson

ANSWERS AND EXPLANATIONS

Multiple-Choice Questions

■ **42. (C) is correct.** He is using the metaphor of water's movement to characterize the movements and actions of humans.

■ **43. (B) is correct.** Jackson is using "fair exchange" in reference to the opposite of the violent and manipulative actions earlier Americans used when interacting with Indians.

■ **44. (D) is correct.** There are five "p" sounds in all, in these five words, and neither of the other options provides a specific enough explanation for rhetorical appeal.

■ **45. (C) is correct.** Though never answered, all these questions require the audience to compare the Indian's behaviors to those of the whites.

■ **46. (C) is correct.** Jackson claims that since they do not have Christian traditions related to churches and gravesites, it should be easier for Indians to leave. This information would help make an argument that locality and geography were important to the Indians.

■ **47. (C) is correct.** By discussing how the General Government is attempting to put the Indians in a locale where they can continue their lifestlye, Jackson's tone is one of accommodation.

■ **48. (B) is correct.** By acknowledging his office, Jackson makes the policies seem less his own initiative; instead, they're the initiatives of an office of government.

■ **49. (A) is correct.** In this passage, Jackson is asking the audience to conclude that by giving large tracts of land to new states that would be controlled by whites, congress automatically assumed that those whites would settle it for their own benefit.

■ **50. (D) is correct.** Jackson here is a proponent of small government, claiming that there is no precedent for the government to protest how states treat Indians, and that states have always had full discretion in relating to the Indians found within their boundaries.

■ **51. (B) is correct.** Jackson claims that his policies will be the best to keep peace among the Indians and the whites, and that even those who advocate for Indian rights would do well to join him in enacting the proposed plans.

■ **52. (C) is correct.** Throughout the passage, Jackson keeps the possibility of war and extermination as a potential outcome that will hopefully be avoided by his practices. He never, however, condemns the practice outright, and seems willing to recourse to it if necessary.

■ **53. (D) is correct.** In referring to warfare and cruelties visited upon Indians as making them "discontented," Jackson is attempting to limit the severity of the fact through less extreme language.

Practice Exams Answers and Explanations

ANSWER AND EXPLANATION

Essays

Practice Exam A: President Bush
September 11th Speech

Excellent answers to this essay prompt will focus on a number of rhetorical strategies used by the President in his speech. Foremost among these strategies is the creation of a sense of unity through a deliberate use of the pronouns "we" and "our." These plural first person pronouns invite the audience to feel a strong connection to both the speaker and the rest of the nation. Another strategy used by the President is antithesis. Apt responses will note the contrast between "these acts of mass murder" and the strength of the nation. This use of antithesis is highlighted metaphorically in the third paragraph when the President makes reference to the foundation and steel of buildings and contrasts them with the "foundation of America" and the "steel of American resolve." Also, successful essays will reference the Biblical allusion found in the penultimate paragraph. Finally, excellent responses will hone in on the speaker's use of diction. Words such as "evil," "terrorism," and "shattered" are used frequently within the passage.

Practice Exam A: Responding to the Synthesis and Argumentative Prompts

The very nature of both the synthesis and the argumentative prompts invites a variety of responses. It would be impossible to capture specific approaches in responding to the synthesis and analysis prompts found in the two practice exams in this test prep guide. However, there are some key criteria that are common to excellent responses. First, these responses will take a clear position on the issue at hand. They will defend the claim, challenge it, or qualify it, being sure to cite specific evidence to support their position. Additionally, excellent responses consider opposing voices. Responses to the synthesis prompt will rebut those sources of information that challenge the specific claim. Those that respond to the argument prompt will, likewise, address and refute potential opposing arguments. Finally, strong responses will be persuasive in and of themselves. They will demonstrate a mastery of language, mechanics and logic. Above all, the very best essays will impart upon their audience a clear and distinct voice, one that adds a level of authenticity to the piece itself.

Practice Exams

Questions 1–15. Read the following passage carefully before you select your answers.

(The following passage is from a history of the 1920's. The passage focuses specifically on the stock market crash of October 1929.)

Practice Exam B

Early in September the stock market broke. It quickly recovered however, indeed, on September 19th the averages as compiled by the *New York Times* reached an even higher level
5 than that of September 3rd. Once more it slipped, farther and faster, until by October 4th the prices of a good many stocks had coasted to what seemed first-class bargain levels. Steel, for example, after having touched 261¾ a few
10 weeks earlier, had dropped as low as 204; American Can, at the closing on October 4th, was nearly twenty Points below its high for the year; General Electric was over fifty points below—its high; Radio had gone down from
15 114¾ to 82½.

A bad break, to be sure, but there had been other bad breaks, and the speculators who escaped unscathed proceeded to take advantage of the lessons they had learned in June and
20 December of 1928 and March and May of 1929: when there was a break it was a good time to buy. In the face of all this tremendous liquidation, brokers' loans as compiled by the Federal Reserve Bank of New York mounted to
25 a new high record on October 2nd, reaching $6,804,000,000—a sure sign that margin buyers were not deserting the market but coming into it in numbers at least undiminished. (Part of the increase in the loan figure was probably
30 due to the piling up of unsold securities in dealers' hands, as the spawning of investment trusts and the issue of new common stock by every manner of business concern continued

unabated.) History, it seemed, was about to
35 repeat itself, and those who picked up Anaconda at 109¾ or American Telephone at 281 would count themselves wise investors. And sure enough, prices once more began to climb. They had already turned upward before that
40 Sunday in early October when Ramsay MacDonald sat on a log with Herbert Hoover at the Rapidan camp and talked over the prospects for naval limitation and peace.

Something was wrong, however. The decline
45 began once more. The wiseacres of Wall Street, looking about for causes, fixed upon the collapse of the Hatry financial group in England (which had led to much forced selling among foreign investors and speculators), and upon
50 the bold refusal of the Massachusetts Department of Public Utilities to allow the Edison Company of Boston to split up its stock. They pointed, too, to the fact that the steel industry was undoubtedly slipping, and to the accumu-
55 lation of "undigested" securities. But there was little real alarm until the week of October 21st. The consensus of opinion, in the meantime, was merely that the equinoctial storm of September had not quite blown over. The market
60 was readjusting itself into a "more secure technical position…"

The expected recovery in the stock market did not come. It seemed to be beginning on Tuesday, October 22nd, but the gains made during
65 the day were largely lost during the last hour. And on Wednesday, the 23rd, there was a perfect

Niagara of liquidation. The volume of trading was over six million shares, the tape was 104 minutes late when the three o'clock gong ended trading for the day, and the *New York Times* averages for fifty leading railroad and industrial stocks lost 18.24 points—a loss which made the most abrupt declines in previous breaks look small. Everybody realized that an unprecedented number of margin calls must be on their way to insecurely margined traders, and that the situation at last was getting serious. But perhaps the turn would come tomorrow. Already the break had carried prices down a good deal farther than the previous breaks of the past two years. Surely it could not go on much longer.

The next day was Thursday, October 24th.

On that momentous day stocks opened moderately steady in price, but in enormous volume. Kennecott appeared on the tape in a block of 20,000 shares, General Motors in another, of the same amount. Almost at once the ticker tape began to lag behind the trading on the floor. The pressure of selling orders was disconcertingly heavy. Prices were going down . . . Presently they were going down with some rapidity . . . Before the first hour of trading was over, it was already apparent that they were going down with an altogether unprecedented and amazing violence. In brokers' offices all over the Country, tape-watchers looked at one another in astonishment and perplexity. Where on earth was this torrent of selling orders coming from?

The exact answer to this question will probably never be known. But it seems probable that the principal cause of the break in prices during that first hour on October 24th was not fear. Nor was it short selling. It was forced selling. It was the dumping on the market of hundreds of thousands of shares of stock held in the name of miserable traders whose margins were exhausted or about to be exhausted. The gigantic edifice of prices was honeycombed with speculative credit and was now breaking under its own weight.

Fear, however, did not long delay its coming. As the price structure crumbled there was a sudden stampede to get out from under. By eleven o'clock traders on the floor of the Stock Exchange were in a wild scramble to "sell at the market." Long before the lagging ticker could tell what was happening, word had gone out by telephone and telegraph that the bottom was dropping out of things, and the selling orders redoubled in volume. The leading, stocks were going down two, three, and even five points between sales. Down, down, down. . . . Where were the bargain-hunters who were supposed to come to the rescue at times like this? Where were the investment trusts, which were expected to provide a cushion for the market by making new purchases at low prices? Where were the big operators who had declared that they were still bullish? Where were the powerful bankers who were supposed to be able at any moment to support prices? There seemed to be no support whatever. Down, down, down. The roar of voices which rose from the floor of the Exchange had become a roar of panic.

United States Steel had opened at 205½. It crashed through 200 and presently was at 193½. General Electric, which only a few weeks before had been selling above 400, had opened this morning at 315—now it had slid to 283. Things were even worse with Radio: opening at 68¾, it bad gone dismally down through the sixties and the fifties and forties to the abysmal price of 44½. And as for Montgomery Ward, vehicle of the hopes of thousands who saw the chain store as the harbinger of the new economic era, it had dropped headlong from 83 to 50. In the space of two short hours, dozens of stocks lost ground which it had required many months of the bull market to gain.

Even this sudden decline in values might not have been utterly terrifying if people could have known precisely what was happening at any moment. It is the unknown which causes real panic.

1. The rhetorical appeal of the first paragraph comes largely from which device?
   (A) Alliteration
   (B) Anaphora
   (C) Synecdoche
   (D) Personification
   (E) Assonance

2. The statistics mentioned from lines 9–15 chiefly serve what purpose?
   (A) A rapid fire series of facts to collectively demonstrate a larger phenomenon
   (B) An introduction of companies that lost money because of bad trading practices
   (C) A retrospective look at what the major industries of the day were
   (D) A characterization of the varied stocks available to investors
   (E) An indictment of particular companies for causing the rest of the market to crash

3. In the context of this passage, what should the reader intuit about the different month/year combinations referenced in lines 19–21?
   (A) That they represented other "breaks" in the same era from which Americans recovered and prospered
   (B) That they were, in retrospect, unheeded omens of the troubles to come
   (C) That they were serious upheavals that changed America's investing habits
   (D) That they were caused by corrupt buying practices that generally went unnoticed
   (E) That they were not important to Americans at the time, and required a historian's expertise to remember

4. The parenthetical sentence in the second paragraph serves what chief purpose?
   (A) It brackets an otherwise incomplete sentence in order to express a particular thought.
   (B) It purveys information that enhances one of the prior points but is not essential to the main narrative.
   (C) It expresses a dissenting view that could injure the argument if not mentioned.
   (D) It dismisses an inadequate explanation for a phenomenon.
   (E) It makes a humorous commentary on the events of the day.

5. Which of the following best characterizes the strategy behind inclusion of the Rapidan meeting in lines 39–43?
   (A) It puts blame on the two leaders for not doing more to aid the failing market.
   (B) It argues that Americans had more important things on their mind during the time of the market crash.
   (C) It questions the importance of peace and naval treaties.
   (D) It proves the author's status as a historian.
   (E) It provides a helpful reference by which his readers might remember an otherwise trivial date.

6. In context of this passage, the word "wiseacre" (line 45) most likely indicates what type of person?
   (A) A humbled stockbroker looking for an answer
   (B) A bemused investor worrying about the market
   (C) An uniformed citizen conducting an "armchair analysis"
   (D) An overconfident, know-it-all analyst leaping to brash conclusions
   (E) A foreign investor with better knowledge of global affairs

7. Given the context of this passage, the quoted passage of lines 60–61 should be read as:
   (A) Nostalgic
   (B) Ironic
   (C) Sympathetic
   (D) Pragmatic
   (E) Paradoxical

8. The phrase "Niagara of liquidation" in line 67 contains which of the following Rhetorical divices?
   I. Simile
   II. Metaphor
   III. Synecdoche

   (A) I only
   (B) III only
   (C) I and III only
   (D) II and III only
   (E) I, II, and III

9. The ellipses in line 122 give what effect to the surrounding narrative?
   (A) They demonstrate an alternate phenomena occurring elsewhere.
   (B) They contradict the overriding narrative.
   (C) They introduce a new perspective.
   (D) They increase the pace and show the process of a revelation beginning to dawn.
   (E) They invite a comparison between the sellers and the buyers.

10. What is the chief purpose of the words "sell at the market" in lines 115–116?
    (A) To quote the advice given to investors by large corporations
    (B) To quote a trader who was interviewed soon after the selling began
    (C) To introduce a commonly held maxim that failed to stop the crash
    (D) To draw attention to a specific practice that caused the crash
    (E) To introduce an idiom that contributed to the economic collapse

11. In context of the passage, what is the ticker lagging behind in lines 87–88?
    (A) Technological advances such as the telephone and telegraph
    (B) The trading happening on the stock market floor
    (C) The newspapers and radio broadcasts
    (D) The mouth-to-mouth news that the bottom was crashing for real
    (E) More modern means of sharing stock quotes

12. The series of questions in lines 122–131 are a prime example of:
    (A) Aporia
    (B) Commoratio
    (C) Anaphora
    (D) Logos
    (E) Pleonasm

13. What best categorizes the author's attitude towards the literal roar from the market floor as mentioned in lines 132–134?
    (A) He feels that the roaring nature of the stock market brought it to an inevitable end.
    (B) He thinks that the roars were okay, provided they did not become roars of panic.
    (C) He feels that panics should have happened more often, and their infrequency posed problems in terms of dealing with economic strife.
    (D) He feels that the roars were an inefficient way to do business, and the market would have benefitted from a quieter system led by a few strong voices.
    (E) He thinks that the nation caused the stock market to panic, rather than the other way around.

14. In context, the word "harbinger" in line 145 most likely means
    (A) Herald
    (B) Commander
    (C) Destroyer
    (D) Companion
    (E) Mainstay

15. What is the main difference between the main portion and the final section (last two paragraphs) of this passage?
    (A) The main portion discusses the economic motives of the investors that caused the crash and the final section elaborates on their effects.
    (B) The main portion introduces an extended metaphor that the final section comments upon and revises.
    (C) The main portion introduces a consistent theme, and the final section rebukes it.
    (D) The main portion provides a historical narrative, while the final section provides an interpretation.
    (E) The main portion and final section both relate similar details, but do so from different perspectives.

Questions 16–27. Read the following passage carefully before you select your answers.

(The following is from a letter written in 1838 by a traveler to the American West.)

If I am here losing the benefit of the fleeting fashions of the day, and neglecting that elegant polish, which they world say an artist should draw from a continual intercourse with
5 the polite world; yet have I this consolation—that in this country I am entirely divested of those dangerous steps and allurements which beset an artist in fashionable life, and have little to steal my thoughts away from the contempla-
10 tion of the beautiful models that are about me. If, also, I have not here the benefit of that feeling of emulation, which is the life and spur to the arts where artists are associates together, yet am I surrounded by living models of such
15 elegance and beauty that I feel an unceasing excitement of a much higher order—the certainty that I am drawing knowledge from the true source.

My enthusiastic admiration of man in the
20 honest and elegant simplicity of nature, has always fed the warmest feelings of my bosom, and shut half the avenues to my heart against the specious refinements of the accomplished world. This feeling, together with the desire to
25 study my art, independently of the embarrassments which the ridiculous fashions of civilized society have thrown in its way, has led me to the wilderness for a while, as the true school of the arts.
30 I have for a long time been of opinion, that the wilderness of our country afforded

models equal to those from which the Grecian sculptors transferred to the marble such inimitable grace and beauty; and I am now more
35 confirmed in this opinion, since I have immersed myself in the midst of thousands and tens of thousands of these knights of the forest; whose whole lives are lives of chivalry, and whose daily feats, with their naked limbs,
40 might vie with those of the Grecian youths in the beautiful rivalry of the Olympian games.

No man's imagination, with all the aids of description that can be given to it, can ever picture the beauty and wildness of scenes that
45 may be daily witnessed in this romantic country; of hundreds of these graceful youths, without a care to wrinkle, or a fear to disturb the full expression of pleasure and enjoyment that beams upon their faces—their long black hair
50 mingling with their horses' tails, floating in the wind, while they are flying over the carpeted prairie, and dealing death with their spears and arrows, to a band of infuriated buffaloes; or their splendid procession in a war-parade,
55 arrayed in all their gorgeous colors and trappings, moving with most exquisite grace and manly beauty, added to that bold defiance which man carries on his front, who acknowledges no superior on earth, and who is
60 amenable to no laws except the laws of God and honor.

16. Which of the following best characterizes the first sentence of the passage?
    (A) It identifies a counter argument that the speaker has trouble neutralizing
    (B) It provides a strong thesis with clear organizational categories
    (C) It introduces an extended metaphor that will guide the rest of the passage
    (D) It dismisses the west as an area unworthy of study
    (E) It acknowledges a criticism, but then identifies a benefit that makes a good tradeoff

17. To which comparison does the metaphor "drawing knowledge from the true source" in lines 17–18 most closely relate?
    (A) To an artist drawing a sketch in order to later base a painting upon it
    (B) To a student reading a great and timeless book
    (C) To a publican pouring a draft of beer from a keg brewed on premises
    (D) To an explorer finding the point where a river begins
    (E) To a chemist creating a never-before-used compound in his laboratory

18. In context, the word "specious" in line 23 most likely means:
    (A) Contrived and querulous
    (B) Hostile and misleading
    (C) Humorous and playful
    (D) Speculative and accurate
    (E) Superficial and false

19. Which of the following is NOT a reason the speaker gives for why the wilderness should be considered the "true school of the arts?" (lines 28–29)
    (A) It shows man in a natural state, honest and simple
    (B) It is untouched by civilization, and bears none of its fashions
    (C) It prevents him from being manipulated or altered by other artist's advice
    (D) It makes him fight for survival, lending vitality to his art
    (E) It provides beautiful models for him to contemplate

20. In context of the passage, which of the following is a main benefit derived from the shift from a singular to a plural pronoun in lines 30–31?
    (A) It argues that we are all brothers and sisters of the same planet, regardless of race or religion
    (B) It opens a formerly personal musing into an opportunity for all to take
    (C) It accuses those who paint in the east of deceptive practices
    (D) It questions the idea and practices of ownership of private property
    (E) It introduces a need for whites to adopt Indian practices of land use and organization

21. In lines 37–41, the speaker categorizes the Indians he has met as all of the following EXCEPT:
    (A) Chivalrous
    (B) Erudite
    (C) Knightly
    (D) Olympians
    (E) Partially naked

22. In context, "romantic" in line 45 most likely means:
    (A) Seductive
    (B) Alluring
    (C) Idyllic
    (D) Historic
    (E) Addictive

23. The phrase "carpeted prairie" in lines 51–52 is an example of which of the following literary devices?
    I. Metaphor
    II. Personification
    III. Malapropism

    (A) I only
    (B) I and II only
    (C) II only
    (D) I, II, and III
    (E) None of the above

24. Which of the following is the best critique of the final sentence of the passage?
    (A) The speaker confuses his reader with a run-on sentence that runs contrary to the rest of his passage.
    (B) The speaker heaps too much praise on the American Indians based entirely on second hand accounts and hearsay evidence.
    (C) The speaker uses a plethora of descriptive phrases to overwhelm his audience in order to parallel the overwhelming experience of seeing Indians as he has.
    (D) The speaker employs a multitude of descriptive phrases to highlight and scorn the differences between Indians and whites.
    (E) The speaker loses his Ethos-based appeal in favor of a Logos-based description of Indian life on the plains.

25. When considered in the context of the entire passage, the word "consolation" in line 5 should most likely be read in what way?
    (A) Mournfully
    (B) Scornfully
    (C) Dismissively
    (D) Disdainfully
    (E) Sarcastically

26. Based on this passage, what audience would this letter be best suited for?
    (A) An artist attempting to find inspiring subjects for his work
    (B) An explorer hoping to know more about the terrain
    (C) An anthropologist hoping to know more about the native culture
    (D) A military officer planning an expedition
    (E) A trader hoping to learn more about economic opportunities

27. Why does the speaker evoke God in the final line of this passage?
    (A) To note an intriguing form of Christianity practiced among the natives
    (B) To contrast the religions of the whites and Indians
    (C) To appeal to the morals of a pious readership
    (D) To demonstrate how difficult it may be to control the Indians by passing laws
    (E) To investigate the differences between the Christian and Indian gods.

Questions 28–41. Read the following passage carefully before you select your answers.

(The following is a speech given to report the death of Martin Luther King.)

Ladies and Gentlemen—I'm only going to talk to you just for a minute or so this evening. Because . . .

I have some very sad news for all of you, and I
5 think sad news for all of our fellow citizens, and people who love peace all over the world, and that is that Martin Luther King was shot and was killed tonight in Memphis, Tennessee.

Martin Luther King dedicated his life to love
10 and to justice between fellow human beings. He died in the cause of that effort. In this diffi-cult day, in this difficult time for the United States, it's perhaps well to ask what kind of a nation we are and what direction we want to
15 move in.

For those of you who are black—considering the evidence evidently is that there were white people who were responsible—you can be filled with bitterness, and with hatred, and a
20 desire for revenge.

We can move in that direction as a country, in greater polarization—black people amongst blacks, and white amongst whites, filled with hatred toward one another. Or we can make an
25 effort, as Martin Luther King did, to under-stand and to comprehend, and replace that violence, that stain of bloodshed that has spread across our land, with an effort to under-stand, compassion and love.

30 For those of you who are black and are tempted to be filled with hatred and mistrust of the injustice of such an act, against all white people, I would only say that I can also feel in my own heart the same kind of feeling. I had a
35 member of my family killed, but he was killed by a white man.

But we have to make an effort in the United States, we have to make an effort to under-

stand, to get beyond these rather difficult
40 times.

My favorite poet was Aeschylus. He once wrote: "Even in our sleep, pain which cannot forget falls drop by drop upon the heart, until, in our own despair, against our will, comes
45 wisdom through the awful grace of God."

What we need in the United States is not divi-sion; what we need in the United States is not hatred; what we need in the United States is not violence and lawlessness, but is love and
50 wisdom, and compassion toward one another, and a feeling of justice toward those who still suffer within our country, whether they be white or whether they be black.

So I ask you tonight to return home, to say a
55 prayer for the family of Martin Luther King, but more importantly to say a prayer for our own country, which all of us love—a prayer for understanding and that compassion of which I spoke. We can do well in this country. We will
60 have difficult times. We've had difficult times in the past. And we will have difficult times in the future. It is not the end of violence; it is not the end of lawlessness; and it's not the end of disorder.

65 But the vast majority of white people and the vast majority of black people in this country want to live together, want to improve the quality of our life, and want justice for all human beings that abide in our land.

70 Let us dedicate ourselves to what the Greeks wrote so many years ago: to tame the savage-ness of man and make gentle the life of this world.

Let us dedicate ourselves to that, and say a
75 prayer for our country and for our people. Thank you very much.

28. In context of the entire piece, what is the primary purpose of the speaker's words in lines 4–6?
    (A) To prepare his audience to receive some bad and shocking news
    (B) To introduce a theme of unity he plans on revisiting
    (C) To antagonize non peace-loving nations, such as the Soviet Union
    (D) To elaborate upon the demographics in the audience
    (E) To draw a line between republicans and democrats in race relations

29. What is the main effect of the anaphora in lines 11–13?
    (A) It demonizes the assassin, and those who would support him
    (B) It questions what form of action is best to take to respond to the question
    (C) It laments upon the hopelessness that is gripping the nation
    (D) It describes the current situation frankly in order to give weight to his solution
    (E) It contrasts the present situation to others that have faced the nation in the past

30. Which of the following provides the best analysis of the speaker's use of the phrase "for those of you who are black" throughout his speech?
    (A) It demonstrates his commitment to being politically correct in addressing his audience
    (B) It celebrates the differences between himself and those in the audience
    (C) It accuses certain members of seeing the world in a damaging black-white dichotomy
    (D) It questions the bases on which racial divides exist by looking at his audience as humans first and races second.
    (E) It focuses on a key demographic in the upcoming election in order to appeal to them

31. In the context of the speech, which of the following can best be said of the words he addresses to his audience in lines 18–20?
    (A) They outline a potential response
    (B) They call for immediate action
    (C) They condemn a course of action
    (D) They diminish the cause for anger
    (E) They question the dedication of the audience

32. Which of the following is most similar to the idea evoked by the metaphoric "stain of bloodshed" in line 27?
    (A) A spot of paint that seems impossible to get off
    (B) A shirt being dyed into a new color
    (C) A fresh wound spilling its first drops of blood
    (D) A patch of mold expanding across a loaf of bread
    (E) A chemical altering the color of a piece of wood

33. The sentence "I would only say that I can also feel in my own heart the same kind of feeling" in lines 33 through 34 is a prime example of what kind of rhetorical device?
    (A) An emotional appeal
    (B) A logical appeal
    (C) An ethical appeal
    (D) A rhetorical question
    (E) An intentional hyperbole

34. By reminding his audience that "I had a member of my family killed, but he was killed by a white man," the speaker is employing which of the following devices?
    (A) Authorial intrusion
    (B) Hubris
    (C) Simile
    (D) Allusion
    (E) Verisimilitude

35. What is the speaker's chief purpose in quoting Aeschylus in lines 42–45?
    (A) To demonstrate his erudite nature and establish credibility as a speaker
    (B) To bring in the words of an expert to corroborate his ideas
    (C) To argue that the nation's present predicament is not unique to their time
    (D) To provide an alternate source for inspiration now that Dr. King is dead
    (E) To urge for clemency for those responsible for the crime

36. What is the chief purpose of the anaphora in lines 46–49?
    (A) To indicate a list of qualities and shared emotions that would greatly help the nation
    (B) To excite his audience into action with heightened rhetoric
    (C) To clearly establish three ideas that he will proceed to counter
    (D) To excoriate his audience for their actions
    (E) To introduce a new idea

37. How might one best characterize the shift that occurs in lines 56–59?
    (A) A conclusion drawn from several clear arguments and facts established earlier in the speech
    (B) A re-dedication to specific ideals that are in danger of being lost amongst the pains of a recent tragedy
    (C) A caution against rash action, based on the speaker's intimate knowledge of past tragedies
    (D) An acceptance of the mantle left open by King's death, and a sort of self-coronation as a new leader into the future
    (E) A musing on the roots of pain and tragedy, with specific attention to the particular details of the present evets.

38. In the context of the piece, the sentence from lines 62–64 should best be viewed in what manner?
    (A) As an identification of the forces threatening unity
    (B) As an accusation leveled at the agents of disunion
    (C) As an inference drawn from life experience
    (D) As a hypothesis to be tested in the future
    (E) As a diatribe about the state of American affairs

39. What is the rhetorical impact of using the phrase "human beings" in line 69?
    (A) It strips his audience of their individuality
    (B) It questions the presumptions upon which all society is based
    (C) It applies a scientific method to a social question
    (D) It reminds the audience of the similarities they share with one another
    (E) It classifies his opponents, by extension, as being inhuman

40. What is the most likely purpose for the speaker's return to the Greeks in lines 70–73?
    (A) It reminds the reader of what Aeschylus had said about sorrow
    (B) It provides a present-day example of a nation achieving unity
    (C) It ties America to the traditions of direct democracy from which it came
    (D) It queries as to whether achieving unity is ever truly possible
    (E) It identifies the present struggle as a timeless one, but one that is worth fighting

41. In its entirety, this document is most related, structurally, to which of the following types of arguments?
    (A) One that uses satire to address a pressing social issue
    (B) One that memorializes the deceased, and then dedicates the audience to the cause for which they fought
    (C) One that questions how the artifacts or traditions of past societies can still have use today
    (D) One that accuses all bystanders, including the audience, of being part of the problem
    (E) One that begins with a clear list of grievances and then provides a solution

Questions 42–53. Read the following passage carefully before you select your answers.

(The following passage is an excerpt from a story written in 1916.)

She was very hungry. Another time she would have stilled the cravings for food until reaching her own home, where she would have brewed herself a cup of tea and taken a snack of any-
5 thing that was available. But the impulse that was guiding her would not suffer her to enter-tain any such thought.

There was a restaurant at the corner. She had never entered its doors; from the outside she
10 had sometimes caught glimpses of spotless damask and shining crystal, and soft-stepping waiters serving people of fashion.

When she entered her appearance created no surprise, no consternation, as she had half
15 feared it might. She seated herself at a small table alone, and an attentive waiter at once approached to take her order. She did not want a profusion; she craved a nice and tasty bite—a half dozen blue-points, a plump chop with
20 cress, a something sweet—a crème-frappée, for instance; a glass of Rhine wine, and after all a small cup of black coffee.

While waiting to be served she removed her gloves very leisurely and laid them beside her.
25 Then she picked up a magazine and glanced through it, cutting the pages with a blunt edge of her knife. It was all very agreeable. The damask was even more spotless than it had seemed through the window, and the crystal
30 more sparkling. There were quiet ladies and gentlemen, who did not notice her, lunching at the small tables like her own. A soft, pleasing strain of music could be heard, and a gentle breeze, was blowing through the window. She
35 tasted a bite, and she read a word or two, and she sipped the amber wine and wiggled her toes in the silk stockings. The price of it made no difference. She counted the money out to

the waiter and left an extra coin on his tray,
40 whereupon he bowed before her as before a princess of royal blood.

There was still money in her purse, and her next temptation presented itself in the shape of a matinée poster.
45 It was a little later when she entered the the-atre, the play had begun and the house seemed to her to be packed. But there were vacant seats here and there, and into one of them she was ushered, between brilliantly dressed women
50 who had gone there to kill time and eat candy and display their gaudy attire. There were many others who were there solely for the play and acting. It is safe to say there was no one present who bore quite the attitude which Mrs.
55 Sommers did to her surroundings. She gath-ered in the whole—stage and players and peo-ple in one wide impression, and absorbed it and enjoyed it. She laughed at the comedy and wept—she and the gaudy woman next to her
60 wept over the tragedy. And they talked a little together over it. And the gaudy woman wiped her eyes and sniffled on a tiny square of filmy, perfumed lace and passed little Mrs. Sommers her box of candy.
65 The play was over, the music ceased, the crowd filed out. It was like a dream ended. Peo-ple scattered in all directions. Mrs. Sommers went to the corner and waited for the cable car.

A man with keen eyes, who sat opposite to
70 her, seemed to like the study of her small, pale face. It puzzled him to decipher what he saw there. In truth, he saw nothing—unless he were wizard enough to detect a poignant wish, a powerful longing that the cable car would
75 never stop anywhere, but go on and on with her forever.

42. The discussion of Mrs. Sommers's habits in lines 1–7 reveals that she typically lives a life of:
(A) Caution
(B) Impulsivity
(C) Abstraction
(D) Remorse
(E) Frugality

43. In context of the passage, the phrase "not suffer," in line 6 most likely means:
(A) Injure
(B) Refuse
(C) Inconvenience
(D) Delay
(E) Confuse

44. What is the main rhetorical effect of referring to oysters as "blue points," and sautéed greens as "cress" in lines 19–20?
(A) It makes the reader feel alienated from the situation
(B) It questions whether Mrs. Sommers is qualified to order in the restaurant
(C) It shows Mrs. Sommers's increasing feeling of comfort with her situation
(D) It paints her as a rude woman who demands speedy service from others
(E) It demonstrates a character flaw that will cause her harm in the future

45. The discussion about the damask and crystal from lines 27–30 most clearly reveals which of the following about Mrs. Sommers?
(A) That she is an imposter, and should not be in the restaurant
(B) That she is forlorn, and needs intervention
(C) That she is entering a section of society that she has only glimpsed before
(D) That she is an experienced woman in determining the quality of damask and crystal
(E) That she lacks the perspective needed to interact with high society

46. The phrase "whereupon he bowed before her as a princess of royal blood" in lines 40–41 is an example of which of the following literary devices?
(A) Amplification
(B) Simile
(C) Synesthesia
(D) Hyperbaton
(E) Metaphor

47. In context, the word "temptation" in line 43 could mean all of the following except:
(A) Distraction
(B) Experience
(C) Sin
(D) Fancy
(E) Enjoyment

48. What can the reader deduce about the other theater goers, given the author's description of Mrs. Sommers in the theater in and around lines 53–55?
(A) They are all critics, there to analyze the play
(B) They are all vain, there to be seen more than they are to see the play
(C) They all lack the degree of new discovery that Mrs. Sommers possesses
(D) They all lack the degree of emotion that Mrs. Sommers possesses
(E) They are all sentimental, putting great amounts of emotion into a simple play

49. Based on her actions and the context of the passage, which of the following best describes the "gaudy woman" who sits next to Mrs. Sommers in the theater?
(A) An unlikely ally
(B) A literary foil
(C) An adversarial figure
(D) A wronged woman
(E) An emotionless husk

50. In the context of the story, the phrase "wizard" in line 73 most likely means:
    (A) Manipulative
    (B) Magical
    (C) Prescient
    (D) Perceptive
    (E) Cunning

51. In its entirety, this passage could be responsibly used for all of the following causes except:
    (A) Advocating for housewives to have more leisure time to spend, and more money to spend upon it
    (B) Attacking the author's society for only allowing those with wealth to experience the finer aspects of life
    (C) Questioning the traditions of a supposedly refined society, and the access that the citizens have to them
    (D) Indicting the theater and dramatic arts for having a corrupting influence on society
    (E) Introducing a form of feminism that looks at women's lives not only in terms of function, but in terms of desire

52. Given the context of the entire passage, why is the phrase "tasted a bite" in line 35 an especially important choice of diction?
    (A) It shows Mrs. Sommers's lack of appetite for anything new, which is a main theme of the passage.
    (B) It mirrors the trepidation with which Mrs. Sommers is approaching the new experiences of the day.
    (C) It demonstrates Mrs. Sommers's fear at being exposed in the restaurant as a commoner who doesn't belong.
    (D) It shows that the high society is really quite rotten, as demonstrated by the quality of their food.
    (E) It accuses Mrs. Sommers of refusing to take risks, and argues that if she lost her trepidation she would be better off.

53. Based upon the entirety of the passage, which of the following best captures the emotion Mrs. Sommers is left with at the end?
    (A) Fear
    (B) Confusion
    (C) Abandon
    (D) Remorse
    (E) Sadness

Question 1: Synthesis

Throughout the past two decades, but especially during the 2012 Presidential campaign, the role of coal production has become a major issue. Opponents charge that coal damages the environment and forces Americans into dependence on a single product, while proponents claim that coal keeps the United States more energy independent and viable as a producing nation.

Read the following sources carefully. Then, in an essay that synthesizes at least three sources for support, take a position that defends, qualifies, or challenges the claim that the benefits of mining and burning coal far outweigh the consequences.

Make sure your argument is central to the essay. Be sure to use the sources provided to help elucidate and support your position. While it is not necessary that you use the MLA or APA format in citing your sources, you should clearly identify those sources that you use to help develop and support your opinion. You may identify these sources by referring to the as Source A, B, C, etc., or you may provide identifying information in parenthesis.

Source A: U.S. Department of Energy
Source B: U.S. Department of Energy
Source C: U.S. Department of Energy
Source D: U.S. Department of Energy
Source E: Senator McConnell
Source F: U.S. Department of Energy
Source G: U.S. Department of Energy

U.S. Department of Energy. "Impacts of Coal Mining." U.S. Coal and the Environment—Energy Explained, Your Guide To Understanding Energy—Energy Information Administration. U.S. Energy Information Administration (EIA), n.d. Web. 4 Jan. 2013. <http://www.eia.gov/energyexplained/index.cfm?page=coal_environment>.

The following information on the impacts of coal mining is provided by a governmental agency.

Surface, or strip mines, are the source of about 70% of the coal that is mined in the U.S. These mining operations remove the soil and rock above coal deposits, or "seams," disturbing land at its surface. The amount of coal produced at a surface mine is not only determined by the area of land being mined at the surface but the thickness of the coal deposit. For example, in Wyoming's Powder River Basin, where coal deposits may run 70 feet deep, a few acres of land may produce millions of tons of coal.

One surface mining technique that has affected large areas of the Appalachian Mountains in West Virginia and Kentucky is mountain top removal and valley fill mining, where the tops of mountains have been removed using a combination of explosives and mining equipment and deposited into nearby valleys. As a result, the landscape is changed, and streams may be covered with a mixture of rock and dirt. The water draining from these filled valleys may contain pollutants that can harm aquatic wildlife downstream. While mountain-top mining has been around since the 1970s, its use became more widespread and controversial since the 1990s.

U.S. laws require that dust and water runoff from the affected area has to be controlled, and that the area has to be "reclaimed" close to its original condition. Many surface mines have been reclaimed so well that it can be hard to tell that there was a surface mine in the area. However, there are areas that have not been reclaimed as successfully.

The following is a document from a governmental agency that reports on the emissions resulting from coal combustion.

The principal emissions resulting from coal combustion are:

• Sulfur dioxide (SO_2), which contributes to acid rain and respiratory illnesses

• Nitrogen oxides (NO_x), which contributes to smog and respiratory illnesses

• Particulates, which contribute to smog, haze, and respiratory illnesses and lung disease

• Carbon dioxide (CO_2), which is the primary greenhouse gas emission from the burning of fossil fuels (coal, oil, and natural gas)

• Mercury and other heavy metals, which has been linked with both neurological and developmental damage in humans and other animals. Mercury concentrations in the air usually are low and of little direct concern. However, when mercury enters water—either directly or through deposition from the air—biological processes transform it into methylmercury, a highly toxic chemical that accumulates in fish and the animals (including humans) that eat fish.

• Fly ash and bottom ash are residues created when coal is burned at power plants. In the past, fly ash was released into the air through the smokestack, but by law much of it now must be captured by pollution control devices, like scrubbers. In the United States, fly ash is generally stored at coal power plants or placed in landfills. Pollution leaching from ash storage and landfills into groundwater has emerged as a new environmental concern.

The following document is excerpted from a government agency's informational website.

The United States is home to the largest estimated recoverable reserves of coal in the world. In fact, we have enough coal to last more than 200 years, based on current production levels. Coal is produced in 25 states spread across three coal-producing regions. In 2011, approximately 72% of production originated in five states: Wyoming, West Virginia, Kentucky, Pennsylvania, and Texas.

Over 90% of U.S. coal consumption is in the electric power sector. The United States has more than 1,400 coal-fired electricity generating units in operation at more than 600 plants across the country. Together, these power plants generate over 40% of the electricity produced in the United States and consume more than 900 million short tons of coal per year.

Besides its role in generating electricity, coal also has industrial applications in cement making and conversion to coke for the smelting of iron ore at blast furnaces to make steel. A small amount of coal is also burned to heat commercial, military, and institutional facilities, and an even smaller amount is used to heat homes.

U.S. Department of Energy. "Annual Coal Report—Energy Information Administration." U.S. Energy Information Administration (EIA). United States Government, n.d. Web. 4 Jan. 2013. <http://www.eia.gov/coal/annual/>.

The following government document offers highlights of coal production during 2010.

- U.S. coal production totaled 1,084.4 million short tons, about 0.9 percent increase from the 2009 total of 1,074.9 million short tons. Wyoming continued to be the largest coal-producing state with 442.5 million short tons, 2.6 percent higher than the 2009 total of 431.1 million short tons.

- Coal consumption totaled 1,048.5 million short tons, up 5.1 percent from the 2009 consumption level of 997.5 million short tons. This increase can be attributed to higher consumption in the electric power, manufacturing, and coke sectors in 2010.

- Coal stocks fell to 231.7 million short tons at the end of 2010, compared to 244.8 million short tons at the end of 2009.

- Coal mine employment was 86,195 in 2010, a 1.8-percent-drop from the 2009 level of 87,755 mine employees.

- Coal mine productivity declined by 1.1 percent to 5.55 tons per miner per hour, slightly below the 2009 level of 5.61 tons per miner per hour.

Source E
Cong. Rec. 10 June 2010: S 4788-4789. PDF.

The following is commentary from Senator Mitch McConnell regarding coal production and the Environmental Protection Agency.

Madam President, later today, the Senate will vote on an issue of vital importance to every American family and business, and that is whether the Environmental Protection Agency should be allowed to impose a backdoor national energy tax on the American people.

This vote is needed because of the administration's insistence on advancing its goals by any means possible, in this case by going around the legislative branch and imposing this massive, job-killing tax on Americans through an unaccountable Federal agency.

Ironically, just last year, President Obama and EPA Administrator Lisa Jackson took the position that on an issue of this magnitude, which touches every corner of our economy, Congress, not the EPA, should determine how to reduce greenhouse gas emissions. But now that it is clear Congress will not pass this new national energy tax this year, the administration has shifted course and is now trying to get done through the backdoor what they have not been able to get through the front door.

Like the cap-and-trade legislation they would replace, these EPA regulations would raise the price of everything from electricity to gasoline to fertilizer to food on our supermarket shelves. That is why groups representing farmers, builders, manufacturers, small business owners, and the U.S. Chamber of Commerce are so strongly opposed to these EPA regulations and so supportive of the Murkowski resolution to stop them.

These groups know these backdoor moves by EPA will deal a devastating blow to an economy already in rough shape. And so does the President. He said himself that his plan would cause electricity prices for consumers to ``necessarily skyrocket.'' The President himself said this plan would cause prices for consumers to ``necessarily skyrocket.''

At a time of nearly 10-percent unemployment, these new regulations would kill U.S. jobs. According to one estimate, the House cap-and-trade bill would kill more than 2 million U.S. jobs and put American businesses at a disadvantage to their competitors overseas.

Closer to home, these regulations would be especially devastating for States such as Kentucky and other Midwestern coal States. EPA regulations resulting in dramatic energy price increases would jeopardize the livelihoods of the 17,000 miners in our State and an additional 51,000 jobs that depend on coal production and the low cost of electricity that Kentuckians enjoy. That is why in the last few days alone, my office has received more than 1,000 letters, e-mails, and phone calls from Kentuckians opposed to this effort from EPA.

A lot of Kentuckians work hard to ensure that our State has the lowest industrial electricity rate in the Nation, and that is something we are proud of at home.

This bill would lead to a dramatic increase in these electricity rates, punishing businesses both large and small.

But the job losses would not stop there. As I indicated, this backdoor energy tax would be felt on farms as well, where increased energy and fertilizer prices would drive up costs for farmers and livestock producers who do not have the ability to pass on these increases. This would be an especially painful blow to them, and that is why the Farm Bureau and many other farm groups oppose what the EPA is trying to do.

There are many different views in this body on how to reduce greenhouse gas emissions. Some favor the Kerry- Lieberman cap-and-trade bill, a significant portion of which, by the way, has been pushed by the oil company BP. Many Members on this side of the aisle have proposals they support as well.

One thing we should be able to agree on is that the worst possible outcome is for the unelected bureaucrats at the EPA to unilaterally impose these job-killing regulations. That is why it is my hope that later this afternoon we will vote to stop this blatant power grab by the administration and EPA and pass Senator Murkowski's legislation to stop this backdoor national energy tax dead in its tracks.

This effort by the EPA would be devastating for jobs and an economy that needs them desperately. It is bad for the economy and bad for representative democracy. It should be stopped.

U.S. Department of Energy. "Coal Production by Region." U.S. Coal and the Environment—Energy Explained, Your Guide To Understanding Energy—Energy Information Administration. U.S. Energy Information Administration (EIA), n.d. Web. 4 Jan. 2013. <http://www.eia.gov/energyexplained/index .cfm?page=coal_where>.

The following map was produced by a governmental agency. It examines regional coal production.

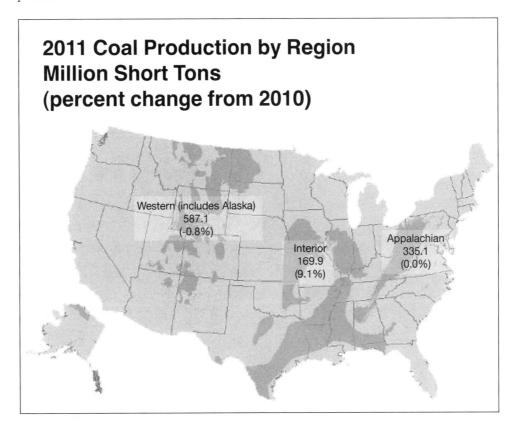

2011 Coal Production by Region
Million Short Tons
(percent change from 2010)

Western (includes Alaska)
587.1
(-0.8%)

Interior
169.9
(9.1%)

Appalachian
335.1
(0.0%)

The following chart is from a governmental agency.

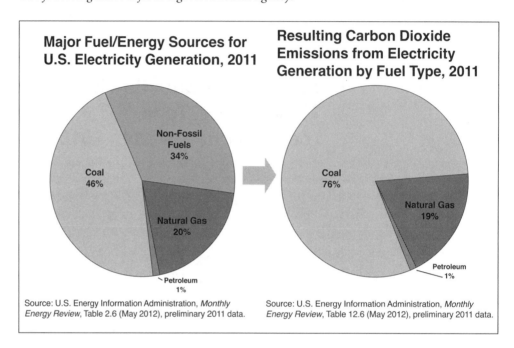

Question 2: Analysis

(Suggested time: 40 minutes. This question counts
for one-third of the total essay section score.)

The address below was delivered by President Abraham Lincoln at his second inaugural address, shortly before the end of the American Civil War. In the speech, President Lincoln contemplates the meaning of the war and speculates upon Providence's role in the war's origin, its escalation, and in its aftermath. Read the speech carefully and consider its political purposes, particularly given the fractured state of the American republic. Then write an essay in which you analyze the strategies President Lincoln uses in attempting to bridge the divide promulgated by the War of Secession.

Abraham Lincoln Second Inaugural Address

Fellow-Countrymen: At this second appearing to take the oath of the Presidential office there is less occasion for an extended address than there was at the first. Then a statement somewhat in detail of a course to be pursued seemed fitting and proper. Now, at the expiration of four years, during
5   which public declarations have been constantly called forth on every point and phase of the great contest which still absorbs the attention and engrosses the energies of the nation, little that is new could be presented. The progress of our arms, upon which all else chiefly depends, is as well known to the public as to myself, and it is, I trust, reasonably satisfactory
10   and encouraging to all. With high hope for the future, no prediction in regard to it is ventured.

On the occasion corresponding to this four years ago all thoughts were anxiously directed to an impending civil war. All dreaded it, all sought to avert it. While the inaugural address was being delivered from this place, devoted
15   altogether to saving the Union without war, insurgent agents were in the city seeking to destroy it without war—seeking to dissolve the Union and divide effects by negotiation. Both parties deprecated war, but one of them would make war rather than let the nation survive, and the other would accept war rather than let it perish, and the war came.

20   One–eighth of the whole population were colored slaves, not distributed generally over the Union, but localized in the southern part of it. These slaves constituted a peculiar and powerful interest. All knew that this interest was somehow the cause of the war. To strengthen, perpetuate, and extend this interest was the object for which the insurgents would rend the
25   Union even by war, while the Government claimed no right to do more than to restrict the territorial enlargement of it. Neither party expected for the war the magnitude or the duration which it has already attained. Neither anticipated that the cause of the conflict might cease with or even

before the conflict itself should cease. Each looked for an easier triumph, and a result less fundamental and astounding. Both read the same Bible and pray to the same God, and each invokes His aid against the other. It may seem strange that any men should dare to ask a just God's assistance in wringing their bread from the sweat of other men's faces, but let us judge not, that we be not judged. The prayers of both could not be answered. That of neither has been answered fully. The Almighty has His own purposes. "Woe unto the world because of offenses; for it must needs be that offenses come, but woe to that man by whom the offense cometh." If we shall suppose that American slavery is one of those offenses which, in the providence of God, must needs come, but which, having continued through His appointed time, He now wills to remove, and that He gives to both North and South this terrible war as the woe due to those by whom the offense came, shall we discern therein any departure from those divine attributes which the believers in a living God always ascribe to Him? Fondly do we hope, fervently do we pray, that this mighty scourge of war may speedily pass away. Yet, if God wills that it continue until all the wealth piled by the bondsman's two hundred and fifty years of unrequited toil shall be sunk, and until every drop of blood drawn with the lash shall be paid by another drawn with the sword, as was said three thousand years ago, so still it must be said "the judgments of the Lord are true and righteous altogether."

—[March 4, 1865]

Question 3: Argument

(Suggested time: 40 minutes. This question counts
for one-third of the total essay section score.)

Poet, critic, and educational reformer, Matthew Arnold wrote in the chapter "Sweetness and Light," from *Culture and Anarchy*:

"If culture, then, is a study of perfection, and of harmonious perfection, general perfection, and perfection which consists in becoming something rather than in having something, in an inward condition of the mind and spirit, not in an outward set of circumstances,—it is clear that culture,
5   instead of being the frivolous and useless thing which Mr. Bright, and Mr. Frederic Harrison, and many other liberals are apt to call it, has a very important function to fulfill for mankind. And this function is particularly important in our modern world, of which the whole civilisation is, to a much greater degree than the civilisation of Greece and Rome, mechanical
10   and external, and tends constantly to become more so. But above all in our own country has culture a weighty part to perform, because here that mechanical character, which civilisation tends to take everywhere, is shown in the most eminent degree. Indeed nearly all the characters of perfection, as culture teaches us to fix them, meet in this country with some powerful
15   tendency which thwarts them and sets them at defiance. The idea of perfection as an inward condition of the mind and spirit is at variance with the mechanical and material civilisation in esteem with us, and nowhere, as I have said, so much in esteem as with us."

Consider both Arnold's passage written in 1869 and its relevance to culture and civilization in the twenty-first century. Defend, challenge, or qualify Arnold's belief that perfection as "an inward state of mind"—the goal of culture—"is at variance with the mechanical and material civilization in esteem with us."

Answers and Explanations for Sample Exams

AP® Literature
Sample Practice Exam B

from Frederick Lewis Allen's "Only Yesterday: An Informal History of the 1920's"

ANSWERS AND EXPLANATIONS

Multiple-Choice Questions

■ **1. (D) is correct.** The paragraph relies heavily on personification; the market "breaks," "slips," and "touches" during it's introduction.

■ **2. (A) is correct.** The corporations themselves are important only in that they are reputable—the major rhetorical impact here comes from the rapidity of the listing.

■ **3. (A) is correct.** The five preceding lines all discuss how Americans had learned lessons from these crashes and benefitted from them.

■ **4. (B) is correct.** While useful to economists, the information is not crucial to Allen's main purpose of showing how Americans experienced the crash.

■ **5. (E) is correct.** The meeting of the President of the United States and Prime Minister of Britain to discuss cross-Atlantic affairs has no importance to this other than to provide a quick reference.

■ **6. (D) is correct.** In addition to fitting the definition of the word itself, the audience knows that there was no one reason for the crash, and that anyone trying to attach it to a British banking scandal was way off the mark.

■ **7. (B) is correct.** Obviously, the market did not revert back to a secure technical position, making this an ironic phrase.

■ **8. (D) is correct.** Similes require a direct comparison, which does not exist here. "Niagara of liquidation" draws a metaphor to a torrent of selling, while Niagara is a synecdoche for all waterfalls, especially massive ones.

■ **9. (D) is correct.** The ellipses serve to show a transition from confidence to despair as prices continue to plummet and those watching the markets realized that there seemed to be no bottom.

10. (C) is correct. Allen uses the phrase as common parlance to introduce a general attitude, not a specific occurrence.

11. (D) is correct. While all the others are mentioned, a close reading reveals that it is the news that is preceding the ticker, not the other way around.

12. (C) is correct. The repetition of "where were the" at the start of each sentence is the definition of anaphora.

13. (B) is correct. Allen never takes issue with the general method of trading as long as it did not become negative and subject to mass hysteria. Indeed, there is a sense of nostalgia for the old way of trading throughout the passage, also indicated in the title "Only Yesterday."

14. (A) is correct. Citizens had expected Montgomery Ward to be the announcer of a new era of economic prosperity, with similar businesses and stores following. This also fits the general definition of harbinger.

15. (D) is correct. The beginning of the passage outlines the facts of the crash's beginning, while the last discuss the fear which, in Allen's interpretation, was central to further spiraling. Fear, obviously, cannot be measured, and is a product of interpretation.

ANSWERS AND EXPLANATIONS

Multiple-Choice Questions

16. (E) is correct. Catlin does conede that he is missing some of the comforts an refinements of civilization, but he goes on to show how the opportunities he gains as an artist far outweigh the relative hardships he faces.

17. (D) is correct. In the sense that he is going back to the most untouched source of knowledge, he is like an explorer finding the source of a river, before other tributaries and terrain change it.

18. (E) is correct. Not only is this the definition of the word, but it is used in the context of decrying the refinements of society which lack substance and give a false sense of empowerment.

19. (D) is correct. There is no hint in the piece that his survival was ever in risk, though arduous; the life he lives is secure enough for him to paint and muse. (He stayed in an Army outpost for the duration of his trip, in fact).

20. (B) is correct. To this point, Catlin has been speaking exclusively in terms of the first person singular. By switching to the plural, he first indicates that there is nothing particularly unique about himself, and by extension encourages others to imitate him.

21. (B) is correct. Though he praises them for their noble qualities and physical prowess, Catlin never attributes the Indians with the kind of classical knowledge to which the term "erudite" refers.

22. (C) is correct. The idea of love never enters Catlin's musings, and he sees the Indians as prehistoric, while addiction isn't the case at all. He does, however, idealize the countryside and its inhabitants as a worry free land.

23. (A) is correct. It might be tempting to choose Personification as well, but carpeted is not a trait usually associated with human behavior.

24. (C) is correct. Though a run-on, the main purpose of the sentence is to overwhelm the reader by providing enough details to recreate the majesty and energy associated with seeing natives in action.

25. (E) is correct. Given the fantastic description he proceeds to give of Indian life, it becomes evident that he thinks it is a great benefit, rather than a mere consolation.

26. (A) is correct. Though a narrow reading, this is also the best—Catlin shares nothing about economy, terrain, or tactics, and only mentions culture as it suits his needs.

27. (D) is correct. He here paints the Indians as entirely detached from western culture, instead only loyal to their own codes and creeds. It would be unwise, then, for whites to attempt to control them in the constitutionally oriented sense to which they are accustomed.

from Robert F. Kennedy on April 4, 1968

ANSWERS AND EXPLANATIONS

Multiple-Choice Questions

28. (B) is correct. The main theme of the speech is about coming together as a nation—thus, by directing his news towards all people who love peace, he makes the event less of an African-American-centric issue (although he also does acknowledge their special right to anger).

29. (D) is correct. What follows next is an extended discussion of the possible solutions they can adopt. The "in this difficult" anaphora clearly outlines the troubles facing the nation.

30. (D) is correct. Though not in an accusatorial manner, Kennedy does make it clear that he sees his audience as humans who happen to be black, rather than black humans.

31. (A) is correct. Though it is clear that Kennedy does not approve of such a response, he does acknowledge that blacks have a right to be bitter, hateful, and retributive.

32. (D) is correct. Kennedy speaks of the problem as an ongoing one, slowly spreading across the nation. This is the same as mold spreads and ruins a surface bit by bit.

33. (C) is correct. Kennedy attempts to assert his authority not only as a senator, but also as one who has also experienced deep grief first hand.

34. (D) is correct. Though not the most subtle allusion ever, this passage does depend on the speaker making the inference that Robert F Kennedy is speaking of his brother, John F. Kennedy.

35. (C) is correct. Kennedy quotes the ancient poet in order to establish despair (as well as the wisdom that can be gained from it) as a timeless issue.

36. (C) is correct. After establishing them as potential outcomes, Kennedy immediately counters hatred, violence, and lawlessness with love, compassion, and justice.

37. (B) is correct. Kennedy is wary that the ideals of love and compassion may be wiped out by this event, and therefore hopes that Americans will say a prayer that the entire nation will not forget those ideals. It is a nation, he reminds his audience, "which we all love."

38. (A) is correct. Kennedy is not naive; he knows that there will still be problems, and identifies them as such. However, his is a positive viewpoint, and lacks the anger and bitterness of a diatribe.

39. (D) is correct. Similar to his earlier use of "for those of you who are black," here Kennedy again focuses on the qualities which unite his audience, stressing their similarities at the most basic and fundamental level.

40. (E) is correct. Kennedy admits that they are caught in an epic struggle, but also implies that they are on the verge of a historic moment.

41. (B) is correct. Both draw heavily on the tradition of Pericles, using funereal moments to comment on the cause the dead had given their lives in defense of, and then arguing that the living should be rededicated to the unfinished work remaining.

from "A Pair of Silk Stockings," a short story written by Kate Chopin in 1916

ANSWERS AND EXPLANATIONS

Multiple-Choice Questions

▎ **42. (E) is correct.** The cup of tea and bite of whatever was around demonstrate a frugal lifestyle, as does her usual self-discipline about actions.

▎ **43. (B) is correct.** In the context of the passage, her impulse is refusing herself the ability to live her own frugal lifestyle.

▎ **44. (C) is correct.** By dropping formal titles and exact wordings, Chopin indicates that ease that Mrs. Sommers is starting to feel as she orders casually.

▎ **45. (C) is correct.** Chopin uses the crystal and damask as tools to show that Mrs. Sommers has crossed through the threshold from the street to high society, and sees the finery in its true splendor as a result.

▎ **46. (B) is correct.** The phrase "as" invites a direct comparison between two different entities. Hence, a simile.

▎ **47. (C) is correct.** This is the biblical interpretation, and it would take considerable irony not found elsewhere in the passage for it to be a synonym.

▎ **48. (C) is correct.** Though the other theatergoers have gathered for different reasons, it is clear that none of them is having the authentic sense of discovery (either self discovery or actual discovery) that Mrs. Sommers is.

▎ **49. (A) is correct.** Given Mrs. Sommers's usually prim and proper lifestyle, it seems unlikely that she would find a gaudy woman so agreeable, and vice versa.

▎ **50. (D) is correct.** It would take true perception of Mrs. Sommers's actions to notice her desire for the day to go on forever, perception so great that would make him wizardly.

▎ **51. (D) is correct.** On the contrary, Mrs. Sommers's time in the theater is perhaps the most liberating, and certainly does not serve to corrupt.

▎ **52. (B) is correct.** "Taste" and "bite" show new experience on the one hand, and a small, carefully selected morsel on the other. Put together, they show the caution she is approaching her experience with.

▎ **53. (E) is correct.** Mrs. Sommers understands that her day must end, and is sad that she must go back to her life as a housewife. She feels no guilt associated with remorse, however, or uncertainty associated with fear.

Practice Exams
Answers and Explanations

ANSWER AND EXPLANATION

Essays

Practice Exam B: Lincoln's Second Inaugural Address

The well-written essay will be sure to examine the speaker's voice and purpose in the speech. The speaker deftly moves through three sections, shifting from a brief analysis of the past four years to an exoneration of the North and mild vilification of the South before closing with an attempt to appeal to the nation, both north and south, as a unified whole. The speaker's diction is aptly selected to place blame squarely on the shoulders of the "insurgents" who "would make war, rather than let the nation survive." Meanwhile, by describing the North as those who merely "accept[ed]" war (as opposed to waging it), and who simply sought to halt the spread of slavery rather than actively pursuing its end in the South, the Speaker is able to portray the Northern faction as noble and virtuous, supporters of a strong union. The overwhelmingly Biblical tone of the final passage seeks to unify the audience, North and South, by referencing their shared Christian beliefs. However, the speaker cannot seem to resist a subtle dig at the South, even as he seeks to bring the nation together. His questioning of the South's audacious request of God to support their quest to wring "their bread from the sweat of other men's faces," somewhat undermines his desire to seek common ground. Ultimately it is tone and diction that drive the speech, and successful essays will explore this in depth.

Essays

Practice Exam B: Responding to the Synthesis and Argumentative Prompts

The very nature of both the synthesis and the argumentative prompts invites a variety of responses. It would be impossible to capture specific approaches in responding to the synthesis and analysis prompts found in the two practice exams in this test prep guide. However, there are some key criteria that are common to excellent responses. First, these responses will take a clear position on the issue at hand. They will defend the claim, challenge it, or qualify it, being sure to cite specific evidence to support their position. Additionally, excellent responses consider opposing voices. Responses to the synthesis prompt will rebut those sources of information that challenge the specific claim. Those that respond to the argument prompt will, likewise, address and refute potential opposing arguments. Finally, strong responses will be persuasive in and of themselves. They will demonstrate a mastery of language, mechanics and logic. Above all, the very best essays will impart upon their audience a clear and distinct voice, one that adds a level of authenticity to the piece itself.